May 8, 1987

Ruth,

It has been a pleasure working with you these past 2½ years. Both personally & professionally, knowing you has been a valuable experience for me. You will be a great asset to your new organization. With best wishes for your happiness & success. Let's keep in touch.

Sharyn

THE MODERN AMERICAN BUSINESS DICTIONARY

THE MODERN AMERICAN BUSINESS DICTIONARY

INCLUDING AN APPENDIX OF BUSINESS SLANG

JOHN BERENYI

William Morrow and Company, Inc.
New York 1982

Library of Congress Cataloging in Publication Data

Berenyi, John.
The modern American business dictionary.

Bibliography: p.
1. Business—Dictionaries. I. Title.
HF1001.B46 650'.03'21 81-22342
ISBN 0-688-00986-7 AACR2
ISBN 0-688-00987-5 (pbk.)

Printed in the United States of America

First Edition

1 2 3 4 5 6 7 8 9 10

To my parents, who taught me the real meaning of business and the importance of markets, and to my wife, who provided the support required to complete the dictionary.

PREFACE

My recognition of the need for this dictionary rose out of my experiences as an active member of the business community when I noticed a wide communication gap among entrepreneurs, bankers, lawyers, accountants, corporate executives, government officials, investors, and other parties; in most cases, each of these persons considers a problem or issue from a highly different perspective. Each individual speaks a "different language," and each lacks the information source necessary to develop a common vocabulary.

Hence, the objective of *The Modern American Business Dictionary* is to provide a reference book for businesspersons, consumers, educators, and business students. The book covers fifty fields and disciplines of business, with the words drawn from those normally used in commercial and industrial arrangements. A separate section on business slang and informal idioms brings together phrases and jargon that are important in oral and written business communications.

Cross-referencing

Throughout the dictionary the reader will find some words cross-referenced.

(1) Words are either cross-referenced within the main part of the dictionary, or
(2) Words are cross-referenced between the main part of the dictionary and the slang section.

Business Language in America

The importance of a comprehensive review of business usage became evident during my academic years at Columbia and Harvard universities, and this awareness was strengthened further during my business career. Consequently, the essay, "Business Language in America," which concludes this book, explores the historical origins of the words, phrases, and idioms commonly used today. As society matures and the speed of change accelerates, newer and more complex words enter the vocabulary of American business practitioners. The nature and context of this evolving language are analyzed and, for the first time, the dynamics of the field of business semantics is documented and explained.

No book of such complexity could be completed without the support of family and friends. My wife, Eileen, provided highly valued advice and encouragement throughout the research and writing phases of the dictionary; the birth of my daughter, Jessica, strengthened my determination that I complete the writing as quickly as possible, since she may want to have a reference source from which to learn these words in the future. A special word of thanks is due to Daiselle Crawford, who typed the various drafts of the manuscript without losing her sense of humor during the long months when the dictionary was prepared for publication.

—John Berenyi
Wall Street Business Publications, Inc.
New York City

CONTENTS

Preface 7

The Modern American Business Dictionary 11

Business Slang and Informal Idioms 263

Business Language in America 271

Bibliography 287

A

abandoned property Property, usually real estate, to which the ownership or rights have been given up or surrendered by the owner.

abatement A complete or partial cancellation or reduction of a levy imposed by a governmental unit. Abatements usually apply to tax levies, special assessments, and service charges, but most commonly involve property taxes.

abator A stranger who contrives to get possession of an estate to the prejudice of the real heir.

able and willing to work Standards generally applied in state laws providing unemployment benefits to those out of work in covered occupations who report to the employment offices on a regular basis.

abrogation An annulment or a cancellation of an existing agreement or statute.

absconding debtor A person who owes money and runs away from his creditors.

absenteeism The practice of failing to report for work for a period of one or more days or shifts, when the worker has been assigned to or scheduled for work.

absolute assembler A program that converts a source program (in assembly language) into machine code.

absolute assignment An irrevocable transfer of title.

absolute error The amount of error expressed in the same units as the quantity containing the error.

absolute estate Real estate or other form of property over which the owner has complete control, possession, and the total right of disposal.

absolute rights Property or contractual rights, which form the basis to enter into a relationship.

absolute warranty A firm guaranty in a contract to which no conditions are attached.

absorption costing Allocating all or a portion (direct and standard costing) of fixed and variable production costs to work-in-process, cost of sales, and inventory.

abstract of title A written and well-documented history of the title transactions or conditions bearing on the title to a designated parcel of land. It covers the period from the original source of title to the present, and summarizes all subsequent instruments of public record by setting forth their material parts.

accelerated cost-recovery system Applies to property used in a trade or business or in production of income. Recovery property falls into four classes: (1) three-year property—includes most vehicles and short-lived equipment, (2) five-year property—includes all other tangible property, (3) ten-year property—primarily all public-utility property, and (4) fifteen-year property—all real property. These classes represent the number of years it takes to write off the cost of property against current income. This cost-recovery system was established by the Economic Recovery Tax Act of 1981.

accelerated depreciation Any method of calculating depreciation charges where the charges in the early periods are greater than those calculated under the straight-line method. Examples are double-declining balance, sum-of-the-years'-digits methods, and the accelerated cost-recovery system (developed by the Economic Recovery Tax Act of 1981).

acceleration clause A contractual covenant which stipulates that a debt will be called in by the lender if there is a failure or a delay in paying debt service or if there are other violations of the contract.

accelerator principle A concept which states a small change in consumer demand leads to a large increase in industrial demand.

acceptance When the seller or his representative agrees to the terms of the agreement of sale, and approves the negotiation on the part of the agent, and acknowledges receipt of the deposit in subscribing to the agreement of sale.

acceptance sampling In statistical analysis and in quality-control studies and procedures, the use of samples, usually selected at random, to determine the acceptability of a lot of delivered merchandise. *See* quality control.

acceptance supplement A document in which a lessee states that certain specified equipment is acceptable for lease. It is generally used in transactions where the lease document is entered into well in advance of the equipment delivery. It serves to notify the lessor that the equipment has been delivered, inspected, and accepted for lease as of a specified date.

access The technical procedures through which files or data sets are referred to by the computer.

access time The amount of time required by the central processing unit of a computer to access data from a specified storage location or to read or write data on an auxiliary storage device.

accident and sick benefits Periodic payments made to workers for time lost from work because of disabilities caused by sickness or accident. This is usually regulated by state laws, union contracts, or company policies.

accommodating accounts In the balance of payments, those accounts that can be considered triggered by the need to finance other transactions included in the balance of payments. Also called compensating or financing accounts.

accommodation note A note signed by one person as the maker, endorser, or acceptor on behalf of another whose credit position is not strong enough to be self-supporting. Usually no consideration is involved. The signer acts as guarantor for the note and offers the credit support required for the transaction.

Promissory notes or bills of exchange made, accepted, or endorsed generally for the purpose of benefiting or accommodating some other individual or corporation.

account Any device for accumulating items relating to a single asset, liability, proprietorship, revenue, and expense.

accounting An information and management-control system conveying information about a specific entity. The information is in financial terms and is restricted to data that can be made reasonably precise. It is used by the owners, investors, regulators, and others in their dealings with the entity.

accounting period The time period for which operating statements, such as the income statements and the statement of changes in financial position, are prepared.

Accounting Principles Board Replaced in 1973 by the Financial Accounting Standards Board, it was the arm of the American Institute of Certified Public Accountants, which rendered written opinions as to the preferred treatment of controversial accounting subjects. These opinions are detailed, include extensive explanation, and are still considered authoritative within the accounting profession.

accounting rate of return Average income from a project or activity divided by average investment in the project or activity. It does not consider the time value of money.

accounts payable Monies owed to a company or creditor that is an account which is not yet settled. Could be past due thirty, sixty, or ninety days or more. This does not include debt or direct borrowing of any nature.

accounts receivable Claims against a debtor usually arising from sales; not necessarily due or past due.

accounts receivable financing Lending which is backed by accounts receivable as collateral. Normally employed to obtain cash, this financing technique is usually limited to less than the total amount of outstanding accounts receivable. *See* factoring.

accretion of a discount In bond portfolio accounting, a straight-line accumulation of capital gains on discount bonds in anticipation of receipt of par at maturity or at exercise of certain call features.

accrual Recognition of an expense (or revenue) and the associated liability (or asset) that is caused by an accounting event, frequently by the passage of time. For example, the recognition of interest expense or revenue for a period even though no explicit interest payments are made.

accrual basis A method of keeping accounts that shows expenses incurred and income earned for a given period, although such expenses and income may not have been actually paid or received in cash at that time. *See* cash basis.

accrued compensation Compensation, due and payable, under the conditions of the employment contract.

accrued depreciation The lessened service value of a facility due to its reduced ability to provide proper service.

accrued interest Interest that is accumulating or has accumulated but is yet to be paid. A characteristic of bond payments.

accumulated deferred income taxes A group of accounts in the balance sheet representing the net balances arising from charges to income equal to the reductions in income taxes of the current and prior periods. Such reduction may result from the allocation, for tax purposes, of deductions which, for book purposes, will not be fully reflected in the determination of book net income until subsequent periods.

accumulated deferred investment tax credit Net unamortized balance of investment tax credits which are being spread over the average useful life of the related property or some other shorter period, as specified by tax law.

accumulated depreciation The sum of the depreciation taken to date on fixed assets. In the fixed-asset account, the balance sheet will usually show the cost, the accumulated depreciation, and the remaining book value of the fixed assets.

accumulated profit The realized surplus or undivided profits usually generated in a fiscal year.

accumulated surplus The fund which the company has in excess of its capital and liabilities.

accumulation bin Where a product or components are assembled. This is usually a physical location used to accumulate all the components that go into the assembly before sending the order out to the production floor.

accumulation trust A trust that uses its income in order to increase its capital rather than paying out that income to a beneficiary or other designated parties.

acid test ratio The ratio formed by dividing the sum of cash, marketable securities, and accounts receivable by current liabilities. Since it excludes inventories, this is considered to be the toughest test of a company's ability to meet its current obligations. Also referred to as either the liquidity ratio or the quick ratio. *See* quick ratio; current ratio.

acknowledgment A formal declaration, attached to or a part of a legal instrument, made before a duly authorized officer (usually a notary public) by the person who has executed the instrument, the execution being a free act and deed. *See* affidavit.

acquisition In corporate finance, this involves the exchange of capital stock and voting stock, and may be effected for cash or cash equivalents such as debt securities. *See* merger.

across-the-board increase A wage adjustment given at one time to all or a significant group of the workers in a plant, company, industry, or government sector.

action ex contractu A legal action taken for breach of promise or obligation set forth in a contract, express or implied.

active inventory Covers raw material, work-in-process, finished products that will be used or sold within a defined period without extra cost or loss.

active market A situation in which the market for securities, futures, or other commodities has experienced a large volume of orders. *See* thin market.

activity charge A service charge imposed on checking account depositors by banks for check or deposit activity, where the average balances maintained are not enough to compensate for the cost of handling the items. *See* average daily balance.

act of God In insurance and legal contracts, a concept used to indicate a danger beyond control of or avoidance by human power; any accident produced by a physical cause that is irresistible, such as hurricane, flood, or lightning, which is in no way connected with negligence.

actual The recording on the books of account, in a given period, of expenses or costs incurred and/or of revenues earned for the period, to reflect the matching of income and revenues to the fullest extent possible, independent of the dates on which settlements of such items are made.

actual cash value The bid price obtainable if the product is sold in the open market. Net of any finance charges, legal expenses, or accrued interest.

actuarial basis A basis used in computing the amount of contributions to be made periodically to a fund so that the total contributions plus the interest earnings will equal the required payments to be made out of the fund. The factors taken into account in arriving at the total amount of these contributions include the length of time over which each contribution is to be held and the interest-rate assumptions on such a contribution over its life.

actuarial solvency An insurance company's ability to meet all of its obligations to its policyholders.

actuary A person trained in mathematical statistics and insurance who is responsible for calculating risks of insurance policies and the associated premium structure required to obtain coverage for such risks.

additional paid-in capital Capital contributed in excess of par displayed on the balance sheet as a separate item, or in combination with par or stated value and designated paid-in capital.

adequate consideration A reasonable and fair price characterizing a transaction.

adhesion contract A contract prepared by a party with a superior bargaining position and submitted to a weaker party on a take-it-or-leave-it basis.

adjusted basis In federal income taxes, the basis used to compute depreciation or gain or loss on sales of fixed or noninventory assets.

adjuster A person who seeks to determine the amount of loss suffered when an insurance claim is submitted and attempts to settle the claim.

adjusting entry An entry made at the end of an accounting period to record a transaction or other accounting event which has not been recorded during the accounting period or has been improperly recorded.

adjustment board A union-management board that frequently operates as the final stage of the grievance process.

administrative decisions Decisions that formulate policy or that relate to applying policies in the daily operation of a business enterprise and implement broader management decisions of the senior leadership of the firm.

administrative expense An expense incurred for the enterprise as a whole as contrasted with expenses incurred for more specific functions, such as manufacturing or selling.

admitted company An insurance company licensed and authorized to do business in a particular state.

ad valorem A tax computed on the basis of the value of the taxed item; usually expressed as a percentage of that value, such as excise, property, and value-added taxes.

ad valorem duties This duty is expressed as a percentage of the value of goods.

advance In real estate finance, a partial disbursement of funds under a note. Most often used in connection with construction lending.

advance commitment A written promise to make an investment at some time in the future usually with specified conditions met, and in most cases requires a commitment fee. *See* commitment fee.

advance dating Conditions that allow for advance dating indicate that the invoice has been postdated to permit shipment of the merchandise. Advance dating allows additional time in which payment can be made and cash discount, if any, can be taken.

advance payment Payments made prior to a contingent or fixed future debt.

advance refunding bonds Bonds issued to refund an outstanding bond issue prior to the date on which the outstanding bond becomes due or callable. Proceeds of the advance refunding bonds are deposited in escrow with a trustee, invested in U.S. Treasury Bonds or other authorized securities, and used to redeem the underlying bonds at maturity or call date and to pay interest on the bonds being refunded or on the advance refunding bonds. *See* refunding bonds.

advance rental Any payment in the form of rent made prior to the start of the lease term. It is also sometimes used to describe a rental payment program in which the lessee pays all rentals, on a per-period basis, at the start of each rental payment period.

advances from customers Receipts of funds in advance of the rendering of the service that will cause revenue to be recognized. A liability account.

adverse possession The right by which someone occupying a piece of land might acquire title against the real owner if the occupant's possession has been actual, continuous, visible, and distinct for a statutory period.

advertising The use of paid media by a seller to communicate persuasive information about its products, services, or organization. Also used in political campaigns and fund raising. *See* public relations.

advertising agency A business organization that specializes in planning and carrying out the ventures or campaigns for other business firms.

advising bank A correspondent of an issuing bank that notifies the beneficiary of a letter of credit or other credit facility without adding its own financial guarantee to that of the issuing bank.

advisory arbitration An effort to resolve specific labor-contract issues in a dispute by an arbitrator, who renders an award that merely recommends possible solutions and is therefore not binding on the parties.

affidavit A sworn statement or a declaration in writing before a proper official, usually a notary. *See* acknowledgment.

affiliate A corporation or other organization related to another by owning or being owned, by common management, by a long-term lease of its properties, or by other control devices. Parties engaged in a specific joint venture may be considered affiliates.

affirmative warranty Affirms existence of a fact at the time a policy is entered into, while a promissory warranty requires that something be done or not done after the policy has taken effect.

after-tax real rate of return Money after-tax rate of return less the inflation rate.

agencies Federal agency securities, such as Federal Land Bank, Government National Mortgage Association, and others.

agency bank A form of organization commonly used by foreign banks to enter the United States market. An agency bank cannot accept deposits or extend loans in its own name; it acts as an agent for the parent bank.

agency charges in media All items, including talent session fees, artwork, commission, and taxes, appearing on the television production budget, exclusive of the production studio bid.

agency commission Compensation paid by a medium to recognized agencies for services rendered in connection with placing advertising with it, usually 15 percent. Some media also allow 2 percent of the net as a cash discount for prompt payment.

agency shop A firm having a shop agreement in which both union and nonunion employees pay union dues; but a worker does not have to join the union in order to be or remain employed.

agent A person authorized by another person or corporation to act for them, who is trusted with the authorizing party's business. One who represents and acts for another under stated terms and conditions including expected compensation. Such a person acts as the middleman and does not take possession of goods.

agent middlemen Business firms—such as manufacturers' representatives and brokers—that are hired by producers and find buyers and negotiate sales, but do not take title to the merchandise. *See* broker.

agent's lien The legal right agreed in advance to payment from a principal for services rendered by an agent. This will include reimbursement for necessary expenditures, advances, and commissions due to the agent from the principal.

agglomeration The process whereby small, usually family-owned companies in the same business but in different market areas are acquired by large, publicly held companies.

aggregate liability coverage The total amount covered by a liability insurance policy. It may cover a specific limited amount for one claim and an aggregate amount for several claims of the same nature.

aggregated shipments Numerous shipments, from different shippers to one consignee, consolidated and treated as a single consignment.

aging accounts receivable The process of classifying accounts receivable by the time elapsed since the debt came into existence for the purpose of estimating the amount of uncollectible accounts receivable.

agreed award An award that appears to have been made by the arbitrator but has actually been arrived at by the parties concerned.

agreement for sale A written document in which the purchaser agrees to buy certain real estate (or other property), and the seller agrees to sell under stated terms and conditions. Also called sales contract, binder, or earnest-money contract.

agribusiness The sector of the economy involved with the processes and procedures of agriculture, including farming, storage, distribution, and processing.

air right A right granted to build above a piece of land or existing structure or building, usually used in cities.

aleatory contract A mutual agreement of which the effects with respect both to the benefits and losses, whether to all the parties or to some of them, depend on uncertain and contingent events.

ALGOL (Algorithmic Language: Algorithmic Oriented Language) An algebraic and logic language that has been adopted by many computer groups as a common international language for the precise presentation of numerical procedures in a standard form.

algorithm A statement of the steps to be followed in the solution of a problem.

alienation Transferring the title to real property from one person to another by conveyance.

alien insurance company An insurance company incorporated under the laws of a foreign country.

allied lines A term for forms of insurance allied with fire insurance, covering such perils as sprinkler leakage, water damage, and earthquakes.

allocate To charge items of revenue or cost to one or more objects, activities, processes, operations, or products in accordance with cost responsibilities, benefits received, or other readily identifiable measure of application or consumption.

all or none In connection with buy-and-sell orders for stock, this term means it is understood that the transaction must be executed only for the number of shares stipulated and no less. In the underwriting business, it means that sales of a new issue will become final only if the entire issue is sold within a specified time.

allotment The amount of a new issue that is assigned or allotted to a subscriber by the manager of the sales organization or syndicate.

allowance for depreciation The accumulation of periodic credits that record the expiration in the service life of buildings or equipment attributable to wear and tear through use and lapse of time, obsolescence, inadequacy, or other physical or functional cause. *See* depreciation.

all-risk policy A policy covering loss of or damage to property resulting from any peril except those which are specifically excluded.

alphanumeric (data) Data consisting of letters, symbols, and/or numbers but in such a form that calculations usually may not be performed on them.

alteration expenses Expenses resulting when merchandise needs some modification before it is acceptable to the consumer. Some retailers provide this service free to their customers; however, the alteration expense may run as high as 5 percent of net sales, and as a result a nominal fee may be charged for alterations.

alternative contract A contract in which the requirements set forth for the parties may be fulfilled in one of several ways.

alternative duties A policy when both ad valorem and specific duties are specified in the custom tariff for a given product. Normally, the applicable rate is the one that yields the higher amount of duty.

alternative obligation Several options exist to satisfy the requirements of the contract.

amalgamation The union of two or more corporations to form a new corporation liquidating the formerly existing companies.

American Arbitration Association A voluntary, not-for-profit organization that maintains a panel of arbitrators who will hear labor or other disputes.

AMEX The American Stock Exchange.

amortization The paying off of an indebtedness through regular installments, such as a mortgage on property, which is amortized over a period of years through regular payments.

amortization schedule A table showing the amounts of principal and interest due at regular intervals and the unpaid balance of the loan after each payment is made.

amount covered In insurance, the amount that is insured and for which underwriters are liable for loss under an insurance policy.

amount of dispute The amount of the dispute not including legal fees and other expenses as related to a labor contract or other forms of negotiation.

ampere The unit of measurement of electric current. It is proportional to the quantity of electrons flowing through a conductor past a given point in one second. It is analogous to cubic feet of water flowing per second. It is the unit current produced in a circuit by one volt acting through a resistance of one ohm.

annual depreciation The annual diminishing value of a property usually tied to the useful life of the facility.

annual report A report for stockholders and other interested parties prepared once a year, including a balance sheet, an income statement, a statement of changes in financial position, the auditor's report, and perhaps comments from management about the year's events.

annuity A yearly payment of money by an insurance company for life or a specified number of years.

anticipation In merchandising with extra or advance dating, an additional discount is allowed to induce merchants to pay the invoice in advance of the expiration date of the discount period. The discount normally allowed for anticipation is the current rate of interest, and is calculated on the number of days remaining between the date of payment and the last date that the cash discount is allowed.

anticipatory breach of contract A breach to perform a provision in a contract even before the contract has gone into effect.

antidumping duties To offset the impact of dumping, most countries have introduced legislation providing for the imposition of antidumping duties if injury is caused to domestic producers. Such duties take the form of special additional import charges designed to cover the difference between the export price and the "normal" price, which usually refers to the price paid by the consumer in the exporting countries.

antitrust acts Federal laws, such as the Sherman Antitrust Act and the Clayton Act, aimed at preventing individual corporations, combinations of corporations, or trusts from gaining or maintaining monopolies and limiting free trade and commerce.

antitrust affidavit A state requirement that an affidavit must be filed each year by corporations doing business in the state. It attests to the fact that the corporations are not part of engaged activities which can be construed as being in the restraint of trade.

APL Problem-solving computer language for handling arrays and performing mathematical functions. Designed for use at remote terminals.

apparent authority The authority granted for a period of time by a principal to an agent to act in his behalf. Such authority must be traceable to the principal, and includes the right of the agent to do only those things that are usually and ordinarily done.

appeal bond One that is filed in court by a party against whom a judgment has been rendered, in order to stay execution of the judgment pending appeal to a higher court in the hope of reversing the judgment. The bond guarantees that the judgment will be paid if the appeal fails.

application package A computer program or set of programs designed for a specific application (e.g., inventory control, linear programming, etc.). In many cases the programs in the application packages are necessarily written in a generalized way, and will need to be modified to meet each user's specific needs.

apportionment A prorated division and distribution of prepaid or accrued taxes, prepaid insurance premiums, prepaid rents, and other income and expenses. Apportionment usually occurs when a property is sold, and is the manner of determining the amounts due to and from the party.

appraisal A valuation or an estimation of value of property by one or more disinterested persons of suitable qualifications. May be in the fields of real estate, antiques, art, and others.

appraised value An opinion by an appraiser that is based upon an interpretation of facts and judgments, which have been processed into an estimate of value as of a stated date.

appreciation An increase in economic worth caused by rising market prices.

apprenticeship training Training that involves learning a skilled trade, and includes both principles and practices of the specific skilled trade.

appropriation An authorization by an act of Congress that permits federal agencies to incur obligations and to make payments out of the U.S. Treasury for specified purposes. An appropriation usually follows enactment of authorizing legislation. An appropriation act is the most common means of providing budget authority, but in some cases the authorizing legislation itself provides the budget authority.

Appropriation Act An act under the jurisdiction of the Committees on Appropriations of the U.S. Congress which provides funds for federal programs. Supplemental appropriation acts are also promulgated from time to time.

appropriation bill A law used to authorize the spending of money and detailing the amount, purpose, and time frame of such expenditure.

appropriation of land For public domain purposes, land is taken away or set aside. The owner usually expects to receive fair compensation for the land.

appropriation of water For public domain purposes, water in rivers, lakes, or other bodies may be diverted after provision is made to compensate in some form those who have been negatively affected.

appurtenant structures Buildings on the same premises as the main building which is insured under a property insurance policy.

arbitrage Transactions made to take advantage of temporary imperfections in the market. An arbitrage transaction does not involve any risk. Because contracts are made, the returns derived from the transaction are known from the beginning, even though part of the transaction may take place in the future. *See* hedge.

arbitration The submission for the determination of disputed matter to private persons selected in a manner provided by law or agreement. Usually the parties agree to abide by the arbitration process. *See* dispute.

arbitration agreement That part of a labor contract or a commercial agreement which pledges as the parties concerned to use arbitration as a means of settling any present or future dispute.

arbitration clause A provision in a contract to submit any present or future disagreement to an arbitrator, whose decision in the matter shall be final and binding.

arbitration tribunal The agency established to handle a dispute submitted to arbitration.

arbitrator A private, disinterested person, chosen by the parties to a disputed question for the purpose of hearing their contention and giving judgment between them; to whose decision the litigants submit themselves either voluntarily—or, in some cases, compulsorily—by order of a court.

area of dominant influence An exclusive geographic area consisting of all counties in which the home market station receives a preponderance of total viewing hours.

arm's-length transaction A business deal in which transaction is open and aboveboard and does not result from some inside manipulation or deal.

arrears Money that is unpaid, such as an unpaid mortgage or a balance which is overdue on a loan.

arson The willful and malicious burning of, or attempt to burn, any structure or other property, often with criminal or fraudulent intent.

articles of incorporation The articles constructed by the creators of a corporation and stating, among other things, the purpose of the corporation, its principal place of business, the amount of authorized capital, the number and names of the directors, and the names and addresses of the incorporators. *See* corporation.

artificial intelligence The capability of a device to perform functions that are normally associated with human intelligence, such as reasoning, learning, and self-improvement.

artificial language A language based on a set of prescribed rules that are established prior to its usage.

Asian Development Bank The principal purpose of the Bank is to foster economic growth and cooperation in the region of Asia and the Pacific by lending funds, promoting investment, and providing technical assistance to developing member countries in the region with special regard to their needs.

as is A term indicating that goods offered for sale are without warranty or guaranty. The purchaser has no recourse to the seller for the quality or condition of the goods.

asked In the money markets, the price at which securities are offered for sale.

asking price In local retailing, the asking price is taken to indicate a willingness on the part of the seller to negotiate the final selling price to some level below the asking price.

assemble To prepare a machine language program from a symbolic language program by substituting absolute operation codes for symbolic operation codes and absolute or relocatable addresses for symbolic addresses.

assembly A group of subassemblies and/or parts which are put together; the total unit constitutes a major subdivision of the final product. When two or more components or subassemblies are put together by the application of labor or machine hours, it is called an assembly. An assembly may be an end item or a component of a higher-level assembly.

assembly-line production A procedure widely used in mass-production industries where the worker performs a single specialized task. The materials and parts are conveyed on mechanical belts, and the worker performs his task as the material or equipment moves past his place on the line.

assess To value property for the purpose of taxation; the assessment is determined by the taxing authority.

assessed valuation The value that a taxing authority places upon real or personal property for the purposes of taxation.

assessment rolls The official listing of all property by address and giving the name of taxable owner, legal description, and assessed value.

asset Anything owned by a company that has value and is measurable in terms of money. Business assets usually consist of such things as cash, real estate, inventory, machinery, furniture, investments in securities, claims for accounts receivable, patent rights, goodwill, and the like. Asset accounts appear on the left-hand side of the balance.

asset-based financing A financing technique which relies on the equipment or facility as the main sources of credit support for a project, and usually doesn't require the general credit support of an institution in order to complete the transaction.

asset-depreciation range Regulations under the Internal Revenue Code that permit shorter or longer usual lives to be used for tax depreciation. Under certain circumstances, capital assets may be depreciated over a period that may be longer or shorter than the applicable class life. After August 1981, assets are generally depreciated under the accelerated cost-recovery system.

assignable lease A lease that can be transferred to another party by the lessee without getting permission from the lessor.

assigned risks Policies issued by insurance companies only because state laws require them to issue such policies.

assignee The person or corporation to whom an agreement or contract is assigned; one to whom real property, or an interest in real property, is transferred or set over.

assignment The legal or contractual transfer of property from one person to another.

assignment for benefit of creditors An assignment in trust made by insolvent and other debtors for the payment of their debts. These are usually regulated by state laws.

assignment of leases The absolute or conditional transfer of the rights of either party to a lease.

assignment of mortgage A document that evidences a transfer of ownership of a mortgage from one party to another.

assignment of rents An agreement signed between the property owner and mortgagee specifically fixing the rights and obligations of each under a lease affecting the property.

assignor One who transfers, assigns, or sets over real property or a portion of his interest to another party.

assumption agreement A written agreement by one party to pay an obligation originally incurred by another.

assumption fee The fee paid to a lender (usually by the purchaser of real property) resulting from the assumption of a mortgage.

assumption of indebtedness An agreement or a contractual commitment by one person to pay the debts of another.

assumption of mortgage Assumption by a purchaser of the primary liability for payment of an existing mortgage or deed of trust. The seller remains secondarily liable unless specifically released by the lender.

at par A bond or preferred stock selling at its face amount.

at sight A term used in the body of negotiable instruments indicating that payment is due upon presentation or demand.

attach To seize, such as to take over property. Usually, an attachment is preliminary to a court procedure determining the circumstances surrounding the property.

attached account An account against which a court order has been issued, permitting disbursement of the balance only with court consent and generally separated from free accounts.

attaching creditor A creditor who has attached, or taken over, the property of his debtor.

attachment A seizure of property or the taking into custody of a person by legal process for the purpose of acquiring jurisdiction over the person or property seized.

attachment of property The taking of property to be held by the court during a trial. This is done so that the property serves as security should the case be decided against the defendant.

attitude A person's lasting favorable or unfavorable cognitive evaluations, emotional feelings, and action tendencies toward some object or idea.

attorney of record The attorney whose name must appear somewhere in the permanent records or files of a case, or on the pleadings or some instrument filed in the case, or on the appearance docket.

attrition A personnel approach providing for a gradual reduction in employment through resignation, retirement, and death. *See* furlough.

auction A sale, generally open to the public, of items and property sold to the highest bidder.

audience composition The number and kinds of people, classified by their age, sex, income, and family status, who are listening to a television or radio program.

audience flow The television household audience inherited by a broadcast program from the preceding program.

audience, primary Television: The audience in the territory where the signal is strongest.

Print: The readers in households that regularly buy or subscribe to a publication.

audience, secondary Television, radio: The audience in the area adjacent to the primary territory which receives the signal but not so strongly as the latter.

Print: The number of people who read a publication but who did not subscribe or buy it. Also called pass-along circulation.

audience, television or radio share of the market The number of all television households that are tuned to a particular station or program.

The number of listeners a radio station has at any time compared with the total potential listening audience.

audit The official examination and verification of accounts for the purpose of providing accurate figures and adequate accounting controls. An audit may be done by public accountants hired for the purpose, or by a company's own employees called internal auditors.

Audit Bureau of Circulation The organization sponsored by publishers, agencies, and advertisers for securing accurate circulation statements.

auditor's report The auditor's statement of the work he has done that gives his opinion. Opinions are usually unqualified but may be qualified, or the auditor may disclaim an opinion in his report. Often called the accountant's report.

audit trail A printed record of transaction listings created as a by-product of data-processing runs or mechanized accounting operations. The record should have the quality of being easily checked or verified for accuracy with convenient reference to source documents and information. Properly designed reports or journals can serve adequately as an audit trail.

authority The right to make decisions and to take action required to complete an assignment.

authority to pay or accept This instrument allows drafts to be drawn on a correspondent or branch of the opening bank in an exporter's or shipper's locality. Depending on the nature of the authority, it may provide for the payment of a sight draft or the acceptance of a time draft.

An authority to pay or accept contains no obligation on either the issuing bank or its correspondent or branch. Hence, the authority may be amended or cancelled at any time without notice. An authority to pay or accept is, therefore, similar to a revocable letter of credit.

authorization (authorizing legislation) Basic substantive legislation enacted by the U.S. Congress which sets up or continues the legal operation of a federal program or agency either indefinitely or for a specified period of time, or sanctions a particular type of obligation or expenditure within a program. Such legislation is normally a prerequisite for subsequent appropriations or other kinds of budget authority that will be contained in appropriation acts.

Authorizing Committee A standing committee of the House or Senate with jurisdiction over the subject matter of those laws, or parts of laws, that set up or continue the legal operations of federal programs, agencies, or particular types of obligations within programs.

automation The investigation, design, development, and application involved in rendering processes automatic, self-moving, self-controlling, and self-improving.

automobile insurance plan A program to make automobile insurance available to persons who are unable to obtain such insurance in the voluntary market.

automobile liability insurance Protection for the insured against financial loss because of legal liability for car-related injuries to others or damage to their property.

automobile physical damage insurance Coverage for damages or loss to the policyholder's automobile, resulting from collision, fire, theft, and other perils.

autonomous accounts In the balance of payments, those accounts that for analytical purposes can be considered motivated purely by economic considerations rather than by the need to finance international transactions.

available funds Funds on deposit with a commercial bank that are subject to immediate withdrawal.

average daily balance The average amount of money that a customer keeps on deposit. It is determined by adding the daily balances of an account for a given length of time, and dividing the total by the number of days covered. *See* activity charge.

average markup This represents the dollar or percentage markup a buyer hopes to achieve for an entire department, for a specific line, or for a group of items. Such a markup may also be planned for a group of departments or for a retail store.

average rate of return The return on an investment calculated by averaging the total cash flow over the years during which the cash flow is received by the investor. *See* internal rate of return.

average stock In merchandising, the average stock = reserve + ½ reorder period.

award upon settlement An award which the arbitrator makes at the request of the parties on the terms of the settlement which the parties have arrived at themselves during the course of the arbitration.

B

backdoor authority Budget authority provided in legislation outside the normal (congressional appropriations committees) appropriations process. The most common forms of backdoor authority are borrowing authority, contract authority, and entitlements.

backlog The total of a business's unfilled orders at any one time. From the manufacturer's standpoint, the ideal situation is a backlog of orders large enough to keep all workers and machines constantly employed, but not so large that the firm cannot meet its delivery dates.

back order An unfilled customer order or commitment. It is an immediate (or past-due) demand against an item whose inventory is insufficient to satisfy the demand.

back-pay awards Unless limited by the parties of the authority, the arbitrator may award reinstatement with the amount of pay lost as remedy and compensation when discharge or wrongful layoffs seem too extreme a penalty.

back-to-back Used in radio or television to describe commercials or programs which directly follow each other.

back up When bond yields rise and prices fall, the market is said to back up.

backwardation A commodity market situation in which prices are progressively lower in the future delivery months than in the nearest delivery month. *See* contango.

backward integration The term refers to a company's seeking ownership or increased control of its supply systems.

bad debt An uncollectible account receivable.

bail bond A bond which guarantees the appearance of a person in court, and which is subject to forfeiture if that person violates the provisions of the bond.

bailee One who has temporary possession of property belonging to another.

bait advertising An unethical retailing offer to sell a product that the advertiser in truth does not intend or want to sell. Its purpose is to switch a buyer from buying the advertised merchandise to purchasing something costlier.

balance The difference between the sum of debit entries minus the sum of credit entries in an account. If positive, the difference is called a debit balance; if negative, a credit balance.

balanced loading Loading a starting department with a product mix that should not overload or underload subsequent departments.

balance of indebtedness A financial statement prepared for a given country summarizing the levels of assets and liabilities that the country has vis-à-vis the rest of the world.

balance of payments The amount of money paid or received as a result of the difference between exports and imports. It is the financial summary of the flow of goods, services, and funds between individuals and corporations of the United States and the rest of the world.

balance of trade The difference between the amount of goods a country exports and imports. A favorable balance of trade means a nation has exported more goods than it has imported.

balance sheet A statement of financial condition of a business organization showing assets, liabilities, and capital, and including net worth as of a given date.

This displays a company's financial status at a given time. The company's assets are listed on the left side, and its liabilities and equities are listed on the right side.

balance sheet exposure Various forms of accounting exposure that differ as to which assets and liabilities are translated at historic rates (unexposed) and which accounts are translated at current rates (exposed). "Exposure" is the net balance sheet exposure of assets minus liabilities which are translated at current rates.

balloon maturity An indebtedness whose full repayment is due all at once, usually at the maturity date of the note, rather than spread equally over its life. Interest payments, however, are usually payable on a regular periodic basis.

balloon mortgage A mortgage with periodic installments of principal and interest that do not fully amortize the loan. The balance of the mortgage is due in a lump sum at the end of the term. *See* variable rate mortgage.

balloon payment The unpaid principal amount of a mortgage or other long-term loan due at a certain date in the future. Usually the amount that must be paid in a lump sum at the end of the term.

bankers' acceptance A draft or bill of exchange accepted by a bank or trust company or other entity. The accepting institution guarantees payment on the bill.

bank examiner A representative of a federal or state supervisory agency who examines the banks under his jurisdiction with respect to their financial condition, management, and policies.

bank holding company Any company which (1) directly or indirectly owns, controls, or holds the power to vote 25 percent or more of the voting stock in each of two or more banks, or of a company which is or becomes a bank holding company; (2) controls the election of a majority of directors in each of two or more banks; or (3) places 25 percent or more of the voting shares in each of two or more banks in trust for the benefit of its shareholders or members.

bank line A line of credit granted by a bank to a customer.

bank notes A note issued by a bank which is payable to the bearer on demand and is intended to circulate as money.

bankrupt A person, firm, or corporation, which, through a court proceeding, is relieved from the payment of all debts after all assets have been surrendered to a court-appointed trustee to protect creditors. *See* receiver.

Banks for Cooperatives The Banks for Cooperatives were organized under the Farm Credit Act of 1933 and operate under the supervision of the Farm Credit Administration. The Banks make and service loans to eligible cooperative associations that are owned and controlled by farmers and are engaged in marketing agricultural products, purchasing farm supplies, or furnishing farm business services.

bar chart A chart, using either vertical or horizontal bars, for data presentation.

bareboat charter party A form of net financial lease relating to vessels. Also sometimes referred to simply as a "bareboat charter."

bargain purchase option A provision that allows the lessee, at his option, to renew a lease for a rental which is sufficiently lower than the accepted fair market value at the time such option becomes exercisable. This is accomplished in such a way that exercising the option appears, at the inception of the lease, to be reasonably assured.

barriers of trade Practices of nations which restrict the international exchange of goods—quotas, embargoes, and tariffs.

base inventory level The normal aggregate inventory level made up of the aggregate lot-size inventory plus the aggregate safety-stock inventory, but does not take into account the anticipation inventory that will result from the production plan. The base inventory level should be known before the production plan is made.

base load The minimum electric load over a given period of time, which is used to measure electric charges.

basic balance In the balance of payments, the net balance of the flow in trade of goods and services, unilateral transfers, and long-term capital.

basic form A package insurance policy providing coverage against a limited number of specified perils.

basic network The minimum grouping of stations for which an advertiser must contract in order to use the facilities of a radio or television network.

basic station A station which an advertiser must include if he wishes to use a radio or television network.

basis The differential that exists at any time between the futures price for a given commodity and the comparable cash or spot price for the commodity.

basis point One one-hundredth of 1 percent. Used to describe the amount of change in yield in many debt instruments, including mortgages.

basket provision A provision contained in the regulatory acts governing the investments of insurance companies, savings and loan associations, and mutual savings banks. It allows for a certain small percentage of total assets to be placed in investments not otherwise permitted by the regulatory acts.

batch processing The technique of executing a set of computer programs so that each program is completed before the next one in the set is started.

bearer The person who has a document in his possession and who will receive any payment that is due on the document.

bearer instrument Any negotiable instrument which is payable to the individual who has physical possession of it.

bearer security A security whose owner is not registered on the books of the issuer. A bearer security is payable to the holder.

bear market A market in which prices drop over a long enough period of time to indicate a downward trend. *See* bull market.

beneficial interest The profit, benefit, or advantage resulting from a contract, or the ownership of an estate as distinct from the legal ownership or control.

beneficiary One in whose interest a trust operates or in whose behalf the income from a trust estate or trust deed is drawn; the lender on the security of a note. Also, one who receives funds from a life insurance policy.

beneficiary statement The statement of a lender that shows the remaining principal balance and other information about the loan. It is usually obtained when an owner wishes to sell or refinance. Often referred to as an offset statement, or estoppel certificate, and is requested by escrow or title companies.

best-effort basis In the issue of new securities, a commitment by the investment banking organization or group handling the new issue to sell the securities as an agent of the issuing party, rather than as an underwriter of the entire issue. While an underwriter buys the entire issue, pays the issuer a fixed price, and takes possession of the securities, a best-effort seller acts as agent, does not take possession, and returns unsold securities to their issuer. New securities sold as "best efforts" will often provide that unless a specified minimum portion of the issue is sold, the new issue will be withdrawn and the investors' money will be refunded. *See* underwriting.

bias The amount by which the average of a set of values departs from a reference value.

bid A price offered, subject, unless otherwise stated, to immediate acceptance for specific securities. *See* offer.

bid bond A bond that a bidder must post when seeking a contract for construction of a public improvement.

Big Board The name for the New York Stock Exchange.

Big Eight The eight public accounting firms considered to be either the largest or most prestigious certified public accounting firms in the United States.

bilateral contract A contract in which both the contracting parties are bound to fulfill obligations reciprocally.

billed weight The weight on the basis of which charges are assessed by the carrier and shown in the freight bill and waybill.

bill of entry The detailed statement by the importer of the nature and value of goods entered at the customhouse and used for statistical purposes.

bill of exchange An unconditional order in writing addressed by one person to another and signed by the person giving it. It requires the individual to whom it is addressed to pay on demand, or at a specified future time, a certain sum to the orderer or to the bearer, usually a third party.

bill of foreclosure A legal request by a mortgagee of a mortgagor to have the property sold and thereby to get the money mortgaged, with costs and interest.

bill of lading A document issued by a carrier to cover a shipment of merchandise. The term is used to describe marine and surface transport, while for air shipments this document is usually called an airbill.

bill of material In manufacturing, a list of all the subassemblies, parts, and raw materials that go into a parent assembly showing the quantity of each required to make an assembly. There are a variety of bill of material formats, including single-level bill of material, indented bill of material, modular (planning) bill of material, transient bill of material, and matrix bill of material.

bill of sale A document in writing that transfers title to personal property.

bill of sight A customhouse document, allowing a consignee to see the goods before paying duties. Such inspection is made in the presence of a customs officer, and is requested by an importer for the purpose of obtaining details that will enable him to prepare a correct bill of entry.

bill of sufferance A document giving a coasting vessel the authority to carry goods in bond.

binary Pertaining to a characteristic of property involving a selection, choice, or condition in which there are two possibilities.

binder, insurance A written evidence of temporary hazard or title coverage that only runs for a limited time and must be replaced by a permanent policy.

binder, real estate A preliminary agreement between a buyer and seller in which the basic price and terms of a real estate contract are included. The final contract is then prepared and signed by both parties. In some instances, the term refers to the actual sales contract.

binding arbitration The established principle that an award in an arbitration is final and binding upon both parties.

bionics The study of functions, characteristics, behavior, and phenomena of living organisms and systems of all species, and the application of the knowledge gained in this study to develop operating hardware, techniques, methods, and procedures useful to mankind.

blanket This refers to the coverage of more than one piece of property under one instrument, such as blanket insurance policy, blanket mortgage, blanket assignment, or blanket survey.

blanket bond A bond secured by all the assets of a company, as opposed to an unsecured bond or one which is secured by specific assets.

blanket contract A contract covering a group of goods or services for a fixed period of time. Such a contract might be agreed to between customer and supplier to allow the customer the benefits of volume discount and an assured source of supply, even though product delivery is stretched out over the life of the contract. The supplier in return gets the advantage of assured business within the stipulations of the contract.

blanket mortgage A lien on more than one parcel or unit of land, frequently incurred by subdividers or developers who have purchased a single tract of land for the purpose of dividing it into smaller parcels for sale or development. Also called blanket trust deed.

blanket order It allows the supplier to furnish special commodities for a certain period of time and at predetermined prices, or on the basis of a formula for revising prices due to market or other conditions.

blanket policy An insurance policy which contemplates that the risk is shifting, fluctuating, or varying, and is applied to a class of property rather than to any particular article or thing.

block A large amount of securities, normally much more than that which constitutes a round lot in the market in question, usually executed as a block trade.

block diagram A graphic display that shows in a simple way the general arrangement of a system or network.

blocked accounts In times of war or other emergencies, the President of the United States issues directives to banks to suspend payment of the accounts of enemy nationals or occupied countries in the sphere of enemy influence. These funds may be released only by executive order or by license under certain conditions.

blocked funds Funds which cannot be repatriated because the local monetary authorities forbid conversion into foreign exchange.

block policy A policy covering all the property of the insured (usually a merchant) against most perils, including transportation. May also cover the property of others held by the insured on consignment, sold but not delivered, for repairs or otherwise held. Usually covers property on and off the insured's premises.

blue-chip stock Stock of the largest and best-known companies in the United States. *See* penny stocks.

blue-sky law State securities laws aimed at the regulation of many aspects of securities industry practice and procedure, from the issuance of new securities to day-to-day procedures in the industry, with particular attention to questions of fraud and deceptive practices.

board of directors Persons elected by the stockholders of a corporation to determine broad policy and maintain control of the corporation.

Board of Governors of the Federal Reserve System This is a government agency located in Washington, D.C., which supervises, coordinates, and controls the operations of the twelve Federal Reserve banks, and has regulatory power with respect to member banks. The Board of Governors consists of seven members appointed by the President of the United States and affirmed by the Senate. Their term of office is fourteen years, and no two members may be appointed from the same Federal Reserve District. The terms are staggered, so that the Board changes one member every two years. *See* member bank.

bodily injury liability insurance Protection against loss arising out of the liability imposed upon the policyholder by law for damages caused by bodily injury, sickness, disease, or death suffered by another person or persons.

boiler and machinery insurance Coverage for loss arising out of the operation of pressure, mechanical, and electric equipment. It may cover loss to the boiler and machinery itself, damage to other property, and business interruption losses.

bond A certificate of indebtedness, in writing and often under seal. Bonds are issued in the form of coupon or bearer instruments, or are registered in the name of the owner as to principal only (registered coupon bonds) or as to both principal and interest (registered bonds).

bond anticipation notes Issued by states and municipalities to obtain interim financing for projects that will eventually be funded long term through the sale of a bond issue. These notes generally carry a lower interest rate than bonds.

bond discount From the standpoint of the issuer of a bond, the excess of the face amount of a bond over its sum (the initial issue price plus the portion of the discount already amortized). From the standpoint of a bond buyer, the difference between the face amount and the selling price when the bond sells below par.

bonded debt That portion of indebtedness represented by outstanding bonds.

bond premium The net amount yielded by the sale of a bond or class of bonds in excess of its face value.

bond rating The classification of a bond's investment quality (the issuer's relative likelihood or ability to pay principal and interest when due), usually by a letter-designated rating (i.e., Aaa, Aa, A, Baa, etc.) assigned by a rating service. In general, bonds with high ratings have lower perceived risks and consequently pay lower interest rates. *See* credit analysis.

bonds authorized and unissued Bonds which have been legally authorized but not issued, and can be issued and sold without further authorization.

bonus plan A payment system to provide an incentive for employees to produce more and thus earn more.

book cost The actual cost of assets purchased or acquired.

book-entry securities A system in which securities are not represented by engraved pieces of paper, but are maintained in computerized records at the Federal Reserve Bank in the names of member banks, which in turn keep records of the securities they own as well as those they are holding for customers.

bookkeeping The art, practice, or labor involved in the systematic recording of the transactions affecting a business.

book value The capitalized cost of an asset less depreciation taken for accounting purposes, based upon the method used for the computation of depreciation over the useful life of the asset. Also, the actual value of an asset after the deduction of depreciation and all liabilities is the net book value.

As applied to an asset, it refers to the amount at which it

is carried on a company's balance sheet or books. As applied to a company, it denotes the amount of stockholder equity, expressed either on a per-share or a total basis.

borderline customer A customer located in the service area of an electric utility system and billed by such system but who is supplied with electric service from a neighboring utility system by an appropriate arrangement between the two systems.

borrower A person who receives funds in the form of a loan with the obligation of repaying the loan in full with interest, if applicable.

borrowing authority Statutory authority (substantive or appropriation) that permits a federal agency to incur obligations and to make payments for specified purposes out of borrowed monies.

bottom line The net income line on an income statement. Used freely in reference to the net profit of a company, unit, or product.

boycott Concerted action on the part of employees and a union to refuse to patronize or do business with an employer.

brainstorming A session involving two or more people during which all ideas generated are scrutinized in order to find a sudden, bright, or an unusual idea that might solve a problem or offer creative options for decision making.

branch store An extension of a retailing outlet, usually a downtown store, that opens a new outlet to compete with other merchants in a shopping center, and operates under the same policies as the parent store.

brand A name, term, symbol, sign, design, or combination thereof, which is intended to identify goods and services of one seller and differentiate them from those of competitors.

brand differentiation The degree of consumer discrimination between products on the basis of product brand, or the ability of a company to promote such discrimination.

brand image The quality and reliability of a product as perceived by consumers on the basis of its brand reputation or familiarity.

brand mark That portion of a brand which can be recognized but is not utterable, such as a symbol, design, distinctive coloring or lettering, taste, or smell.

brand name That part of a brand which can be vocalized. This could include words, numbers, or initials.

breach of contract The failure, without legal excuse, to fulfill any promise which forms the whole or part of a contract.

breach of trust Any act done by a trustee contrary to the terms of his trust, or in excess of his authority and to the detriment of the trust.

break-even chart A graphic tool showing the total variable-cost and fixed-cost curve along with the total revenue (gross income) curve, both at all possible outputs. The point of intersection is defined as the break-even point; i.e., the point where revenues just equal costs.

break-even point In residential or commercial property, the figure at which occupancy income is equal to all required expenses and debt service.

The amount of sales necessary for a company, financial project, or product to recover all associated costs. The break-even point is when total revenue equals fixed costs plus variable costs.

break-even-point analysis Charting and analyzing relationships, usually between sales and expenses, to determine at what size or volume an operation breaks even between a loss or a profit; such analysis can be used in any problem area where marginal effects can be pinpointed.

bridge financing Interim financing between the start of operation and the obtaining of long-term financing.

British Thermal Unit (BTU) The standard unit for measuring a quantity of heat energy, such as the heat content of fuel. It is the amount of heat necessary to raise the temperature of one pound of water one degree Fahrenheit.

broker An independent intermediary between buyer and seller who brings parties together to facilitate the conclusion of sales contracts. The broker does not necessarily have a continuous relationship with his principals, even though they may frequently call on his services. He charges a fee for his assistance and is sometimes called a "selling agent." *See* agent middlemen.

brokers' loans Money borrowed by brokers from banks or other brokers for a variety of uses. It may be used by specialists to help finance inventories of stock they deal in, and by brokerage firms to finance the underwriting of new issues of corporate and municipal securities. It may also be used to help finance a firm's own investments, and to help finance the purchase of securities for customers who prefer to use a broker's credit when they buy securities.

budget A projection of future income, expenses, and profit. A standard against which to measure performance for management control.

budgetary control The control or management of a governmental unit or enterprise in accordance with an approved budget for the purpose of keeping expenditures within the limitations or available appropriations and available revenues.

budget authority The authority provided by law to enter into obligations which will result in immediate or future outlays involving government funds, except that such a term does not include the authority to insure or guarantee the repayment of indebtedness incurred by another person or government. The basic forms of budget authority are appropriations, contract authority, and borrowing authority.

budgeting Projecting and planning a company's or a government's revenues, expenses, and capital requirements for a future period. Usually broken down into an operating or a profit-center unit, such a procedure allows for: (1) top policy makers' concurrence with the included plans and projections; (2) a periodic evaluation of how successful each unit is in meeting its sales, service delivery, and cost goals; and (3) administering prompt corrective action where necessary. It is a tool for translating policy objectives and strategic goals into concrete actions.

budgeting amendment A formal request submitted to the U.S. Congress by the President, after his formal budget transmittal but prior to completion of appropriation action by the Congress, that revises previous requests, such as the amount of budget authority.

budget message A discussion of the proposed budget presented in writing by the budget-making authority to the legislative body. The budget message should contain an explanation of the principal budget items, an outline of the governmental unit's experience during the past period and its financial status at the time of the message, and recommendations regarding the financial policy for the coming period.

budget system A system by which income and expenditure for a definite period are balanced.

budget update A statement summarizing amendments to or revisions in the budget authority requested, estimated outlays, and estimated receipts for a fiscal year that has not been completed.

building loan An agreement by which a lender undertakes to advance to a contractor money to be used primarily in the erection of buildings.

building permit A written document, issued by a town, city, or county, allowing one to build a proposed structure. The permit is issued in accordance with zoning requirements of the local government.

bulk mailing A quantity of third-class mail that must be delivered to the post office in bundles, sorted by state and city.

bulk storage Large-scale storage vessels for raw materials, intermediate goods, or finished products in the process industries. Each vessel normally contains a mixture of lots, and materials may be replenished and withdrawn for use or pack-out simultaneously.

bull market A market in which prices rise over a long enough period of time to indicate an upward trend; normally used to describe trends measured in months or years rather than short-term swings. *See* bear market.

bumping The procedure used during layoffs in which an employee with greater seniority has the right to displace an employee of lesser seniority.

burdensome buy out A provision in a lease allowing the lessee to purchase leased property at a value to be determined in some fashion when the buy out is exercised if and whenever payments under the tax or general-indemnity clauses are considered unusually burdensome by the lessee.

burglary and theft insurance Insurance against loss or damage to property. Term commonly includes burglary, theft, and robbery insurance, and often refers to insurance against the loss of money or securities due to any cause.

buried offer An offer for a booklet, sample, or information made by a statement within the text of an advertisement without the use of a coupon or typographical emphasis. Also called hidden offer.

business agent A representative of a labor union. Usually he is a paid member of the union staff who visits various union shops to hear comments and grievances from the workers.

business cycle The fluctuation of business activity during which the stages of recovery, prosperity, recession, and depression are observed. Some cycles may have a period of severe depression between prosperity and recession.

business expense The expense in carrying on business. A usual or customary expenditure in the course of business during the year, which is deductible from income taxes.

business interruption insurance Protection for a business owner against losses resulting from a temporary shutdown because of fire or other insured peril. The insurance provides reimbursement for lost net profits and for necessary continuing expenses.

business machine A machine designed to facilitate clerical operations in commercial or scientific activities.

Business Publications Audit of Circulation, Inc. (BPA) An auditing organization for business publications which are primarily concerned with controlled circulation.

business risk That component of a company's overall risk which is associated with its ability to compete successfully in the marketplace.

buyer In retail business, an individual who undertakes the purchase and stocking of various items for the store. Buyers are generally associated with department or chain stores rather than with small independent stores, where the owner or manager performs this function.

buyer's market A market in which supply is greater than demand, giving buyers considerable influence over prices and terms of sales. Prices generally tend to move downward in a buyer's market. *See* seller's market.

buyer's option The privilege of buying a commodity, security, merchandise, or other property within a given period of time, usually at a price and under conditions agreed upon in advance of the actual sale.

buying services for media Professional organizations that plan and execute media schedules for agencies and advertisers. Also known as media services, operating chiefly in the broadcast field.

buying space Buying the right to insert an advertisement in a given medium, such as a periodical, a program, or an outdoor sign; buying time is the corresponding term for the purchase of television or radio broadcast privileges.

buyout policy A professional insurance policy covering future claims resulting from incidents that occurred during the period an expired claims-made policy was in force.

buy-sell agreement An agreement whereby owners of a business arrange to transfer their respective ownership interests upon the death of one of the owners or upon some other event, so as to provide continued control of the business or some other desired goal.

bylaws Regulations, ordinances, rules, or laws adopted by an association or corporation or a similar entity for its government. The word has also been used to designate the local laws or municipal statutes of a city or town.

by-product A material of value which results as a sidestream of a production process. The ratio of by-product to primary product is usually fixed. By-products may be recycled, sold as is, or used for other purposes.

by-product power Power generated in conjunction with an industrial process which optimizes or matches the generation of electricity to the steam and/or heat requirements.

byte The smallest addressable unit of data storage in a computer.

C

call A stock option to buy a certain security, usually a round lot, at a specified price within a specified period of time. A call would be purchased by someone who thinks the market price of a particular stock will increase above the call price during the life of the call. The owner would thus make a profit equal to the difference between the two prices (less the price of the call). *See* put, option.

callable bond A bond for which the issuer reserves the right to pay the obligation before maturity date. If the issuer agrees to pay more than the face amount of the bond when called, the excess of the payment over the face amount is the call premium.

call money Money loaned by banks to brokers that is subject to call (demand payment) at the discretion of the lender.

call premium The amount of the premium payment due a bondholder when a callable bond is redeemed before maturity by its issuer, as specified by the terms of the bond issue. That amount may vary with redemption date, the premium diminishing as the bond matures.

call price The price paid for a security when it is called (i.e., when the call provision is exercised). The call price is equal to the face value of the security plus the call premium.

call provision In a mortgage or deed of trust, a clause giving the mortgagee or beneficiary the right to accelerate payment of the mortgage debt in full on a certain date or upon the development of specified conditions.

A provision in the terms of a security which permits the issuer to redeem it at a specified price (generally higher than the face value) after a specified length of time.

cancelled checks Checks which have been paid and charged to the depositor's account, then perforated with the date of the payment and the drawee bank's name or clearinghouse number. These checks are retained in the files of the bank until a statement of the depositor's account is sent to him, at which time the cancelled checks are submitted for his acceptance and approval.

capacity The highest sustainable output rate which can be achieved with the current product specifications, product mix, work force, plant, and equipment.

capacity to insure A measure of the amount of coverage which an insurance company is able or prepared to assume on particular risks.

capacity planning The measurement of the volume of work that can be processed with given resources.

capital The money and/or property comprising the wealth owned or used by a person or business enterprise. The accumulated wealth of a person or business. The net worth of a business represented by the amount that its assets exceed its liabilities.

capital account In the balance of payments, the section that records the changes in financial assets and liabilities. The capital account is divided into two major sections: long-term flows and short-term flows.

capital asset A tangible asset whose benefit is to be used over a period of time rather than in the period of acquisition.

capital budget A systematic plan of proposed capital outlays and the means of financing them for a fiscal period.

capital gain The excess of proceeds over cost from the sale of a capital asset.

capital goods Equipment, machinery, or tools which are used in the production of, or facilitate the eventual production of, other goods. In general, they comprise that portion of industrial goods which are not consumed in the normal course of business.

capitalization The underlying value of a company represented by the total amount of all types of securities issued by it and its subsidiaries. A company's capitalization may consist of any mix of bonds, debentures, long-term debt, and preferred and common stocks.

capitalization rate The percentage rate at which an anticipated future income stream from an investment is discounted to present worth (i.e., market value).

capitalize To raise funds for investment in a business by issuing securities; or to include in any asset account an expenditure which will provide future benefits, thus postponing recognition of an expense until the associated income benefits are realized. *See* equity capital.

capital lease Generally transfers ownership to the lessee at the end of the lease term, and contains an option to purchase property at a bargain price.

capital market The market composed of the buyers, sellers, and issuers of securities (both debt and equity). It is composed of institutions, banks, governments, corporations, and the investing public. Transactions may be executed in organized exchanges or over-the-counter via telephone.

capital program A plan for capital expenditures to be incurred each year over a fixed period of years to meet capital needs arising from the long-term work program. It designates each project or other contemplated expenditure in which the corporation or government is to have a part and specifies the full resources estimated to be available to finance the projected expenditures.

capital stock The ownership shares of a corporation authorized by its articles of incorporation.

capital stock insurance company A company having in addition to surplus and reserve funds a capital fund paid in by stockholders.

capital structure The composition of the various types of securities issued by a company which is usually measured in terms of the proportion of debt or equity to total outstanding capital. Such a measure often determines a company's ability to issue additional debt or equity under favorable terms.

capital surplus The capital invested in a business by the owners or stockholders over and above the legal capital requirement. It is the difference between the issuing price and the par value of a company's common stock. *See* paid-in surplus.

capital turnover The ratio between net sales and the average inventory at cost.

captive insurer An insurance company set up by a company or a group of companies to insure their own risks or risks common to the group.

cargo The freight transported in a vehicle.

cargo insurance Insurance covering goods being transported by some conveyance, such as a ship, train, or truck.

carrying charges Any normal and repeated charge stemming from asset ownership, such as interest charged by brokers on margin accounts and charges for warehousing goods.

carrying cost The cost of carrying inventory, usually defined as a percentage of the dollar value of inventory per unit of time (generally one year). Depends mainly on the cost of capital invested as well as on the costs of maintaining the inventory, such as taxes and insurance, obsolescence, spoilage, and space occupied.

cartel An association of industrial or business concerns whose purpose is to corner a market or to fix prices or to acquire a monopoly in a specific field. Cartels are often secret and sometimes illegal. *See* monopoly.

cash Currently, coins, checks, postal and express money orders, and bankers' drafts on hand or on deposit with an official or agent designated as custodian of cash and bank deposits.

cash basis An accounting treatment under which revenues are recorded when received in cash, and expenditures are recorded when paid. *See* accrual basis.

cash budget The budget or schedule of a company's cash position, including inflows, outflows, and net cash based over a period of time.

cash contract A contract that does not create a debt because the contract is fulfilled and settled with the payment of cash.

cash discount A deduction from billed price which a seller allows for payment within a certain time.

cash flow The spendable income from an investment after subtracting from the gross income all operating expenses, loan payments, and the allowance for the income tax attributed to the income. The amount of cash derived over a period of time from the operation of income-producing property after debt services and operating expenses, but before depreciation and income taxes.

cash-flow statement A statement of cash income and outgo between two given dates.

cash forecast An estimate of the amount of cash expected to be received in a given period of time, the amount to be spent, and the anticipated balance on hand at the end of the period.

cashier's check A bank's own check drawn on itself and signed by the cashier or another authorized official. It is a direct responsibility of the bank. It is used to pay obligations of the bank; to disburse the proceeds of a loan to the borrower in lieu of credit to his deposit account; and it is sold to customers for domestic remittance purposes when a personal check is not acceptable.

cash in advance When the seller receives payment before shipping the goods. Used for small shipments or for the sale of goods which have to be specially manufactured for a highly specialized end use.

cash item Any item immediately convertible into cash. The term also includes all items not in the form of cash, which are held in a general ledger account titled "Cash Items" pending conversion into cash.

cash management A financial tool used by corporations, investment and portfolio managers, and individuals in structuring an investment program best suited for the cash-flow needs of the investor or corporation. The liquidity, maturity, and credit quality of the investments in the portfolio are considerations in establishing a cash-management program.

cash-management bill Very short-maturity bills that the U.S. Treasury occasionally sells because its cash balances are down and it needs money for a few days. The sale is usually prior to revenues to be received by the U.S. Treasury.

cash market Denotes the market in which commodities were traded against cash for immediate delivery, in contrast to delivery in the futures market.

cash-on-cash return The direct rate of return on an investment measured by the cash returned to the investor, based on the investor's cash investment without regard to income tax savings or the use and cost of the borrowed funds.

cash settlement In the money market, a transaction is made for cash settlement if the securities purchased are delivered against payment in federal funds on the same day the trade is made.

cash surrender value The value of an insurance policy at any specific time before the policy is due. The cash surrender value of a life policy is the reserve less a surrender charge.

cash value The amount for which something can be sold in a free market. Also known as market value, fair market value.

casualty insurance The coverage of loss or liability arising from accidents or mishaps, excluding certain types of loss which by law or custom are considered as falling exclusively within the scope of other types of insurance like fire or marine.

catastrophe In insurance, a term applied for statistical recording purposes to an incident or a series of related incidents involving an insured loss expected to exceed a million dollars.

cathode-ray tube A television-like screen on which information is flashed that relates to current data required for processing an order.

centralization Decision making is reserved for a few individuals in the organization. *See* decentralization.

centralization of authority The policy to restrict the delegation of decision making in an organizational structure, usually by holding it at or near the top of the organizational strucure. *See* decentralization of authority.

centralized government authority Exists in government-controlled economic systems where almost all business decisions are made by a central government agency.

central processing unit A unit of a computer which includes the circuits controlling the interpretation and execution of instructions.

certificate of acceptance A document whereby the borrower or renter acknowledges that the property or equipment to be delivered to him is acceptable to him, and has been manufactured or constructed in accordance with specifications.

certificate of deposit A receipt for a bank deposit in certificate rather than passbook form. Time certificates of deposit are payable either on a specific date or after the passage of a specific amount of time; they can bear interest and are therefore widely used by companies and institutions as short-term investment vehicles.

certificate of incorporation The franchise or charter issued by a state to the original petitioners of an approved corporation. Such a franchise or charter constitutes the authority granted by the state for the organization to transact business as a corporation.

certificate of occupancy Written authorization given by a local municipality that allows a newly completed or a substantially completed structure to be inhabited after the building meets all local ordinances and regulations.

certificate of origin A certificate issued by the proper authorities which accompanies the documents attached to a draft covering the shipment of goods. The certificate usually specifies the origin of material or labor used in the production of such merchandise.

certificate of sale A certificate issued to the purchaser at a judicial sale, as in the case of a mortgage foreclosure by the court.

certificate of title A statement furnished by an abstract or title company or by an attorney to a client stating that the title to a piece of property is legally vested in the present owner. *See* title insurance.

certification mark A name or design used upon, or in connection with, the products or services of persons other than the owner of the mark, to certify origin, material, mode of manufacture, quality, accuracy, or other characteristics of such goods or services.

certified check A depositor's check recognized and accepted by a bank officer as a valid appropriation of the amount specified and as drawn against funds held by bank.

certified copy A copy of a document or record, signed and certified as a true copy by the officer to whose custody the original is entrusted.

certified financial statement A final statement attested to by an independent public auditor who is a certified public accountant.

certified public accountant An accountant to whom a state has granted a certificate showing that he has met prescribed educational experience and examination requirements designed to ensure competence in the practice of public accounting. The accountant holding such a certificate is permitted to use the designation Certified Public Accountant, commonly abbreviated to C.P.A.

chain A band of radio frequencies assigned to a given radio or television station or for other broadcasting purposes.

chain of title Documentation of various transfers of title to property from one person to another, commencing from the earliest records of ownership and terminating with the deed to the person presently claiming title.

chain store A store under the control of central ownership which stocks and distributes similar lines of goods.

change of title The transfer of property from one person or corporation to another, with the purchaser assuming title.

channel of distribution The established route a product follows to reach the final consumer. This will involve agents, dealers, and wholesalers before it reaches the retail establishment. *See* marketing channel.

chapter XI A financial and legal condition of an enterprise that has gone into bankruptcy. Under bankruptcy laws, such a company may be permitted by the court to continue to do business for a time so long as it pays all its current debts. It must move out from "Chapter XI" eventually through reorganization, or it must cease doing business.

charge-off Anything manifesting intent to eliminate an item from assets.

charter An act of a legislature or a government agency creating a corporation and setting forth its franchise; also, a document defining the organization of a corporation, usually created by the corporation.

charter party A document which provides for the lease of a vessel. The format is basically the same as any other lease. There are certain additions and modifications in order to reflect the requirements dictated by a vessel transaction.

chart of accounts A list of accounting titles showing the order of arrangement and the classification of accounts in the general ledger.

chattel mortgage A transfer of some legal or equitable right in personal property, or the creation of a lien on it, as security for the payment of money or for performance of some other act.

cheap money A financial condition when the value of a particular currency is low compared with the value of goods and services. It describes a situation when the general price level is high and a relatively small amount of goods or services can be obtained for a relatively large quantity of money. Also, cheap money is money lent at low interest rates.

check A commercial device intended for use as a temporary expedient for actual money, and generally designed for immediate payment and not for circulation.

check-off system Deduction of certain sums by an employer from the pay of employees and payment of such sums to the union.

child labor laws Laws and regulations prohibiting the employment of minors under a specified age. The age may vary from state to state.

circulation Refers to the number of people a medium reaches. (1) In publication advertising, the prime circulation is that which is paid for by the readers, in contrast to pass-along circulation; (2) in outdoor and transportation advertising, the term refers to people who have a reasonable opportunity to read the display; (3) in television, it usually means the audience.

claim The formal demand for payment for a loss under the terms of an insurance contract.

classified advertising One of the two broad divisions of advertising in newspapers and magazines. It appears in special columns on pages where advertising is assembled by product or service.

class magazines Publications that reach select high-income readers, in contrast to magazines of larger circulations, generally referred to as mass magazines.

clean credit A commercial letter of credit which does not require the usual type of documents generally required. These letters are used for penalty payments, to support contract bids, to provide for periodic payments, and for other purposes.

clearinghouse An association of banks, organized at one place such as New York, to exchange checks and other types of indebtedness held by one member bank that originated from another. It is an intermediary for the debts and credits of its members.

clearinghouse funds Payments made through the New York Clearing House's computerized Clearing House Interbank Payments Systems. Clearinghouse debits and credits are settled in federal funds on the first business day after clearing.

clear title Good title, marketable title, one free from encumbrance, obstruction, burden, limitation, or objection.

close To transfer the balance of a temporary or adjunct account to the main account to which it relates; for example, to transfer revenue and expense accounts directly, or to transfer purchase discounts to purchases.

closed corporation A closed corporation is one in which the directors and officers have the power to fill vacancies in their own group, without allowing to the general body of stockholders any choice or vote in their election.

closed-end question A type of question which elicits a direct answer from respondents. Uses a structured questionnaire. *See* open-end question.

closed period That portion of the term of a mortgage loan during which the loan cannot be prepaid.

closed shop A company in which an employee must be a member of the union before he can be hired or continue employment. *See* open shop.

closed-shop contract A contract requiring an employer to hire only union members and to discharge nonunion members, and requiring that employees, as a condition of employment, remain union members.

closing The conclusion or consummation of a transaction. In real estate, closing includes the delivery of a deed, title report, financial adjustments, the signing of notes, and the disbursement of funds necessary to the sale or loan transaction.

closing costs All of the costs to the buyer and seller individually that are associated with the purchase, sale, or financing of real property. These include but are not limited to the prorating of agreed items such as taxes and rents, the cost of title-insurance policies, the cost of credit reports, recording fees, and escrow fees.

closing statement A financial disclosure given to the buyer and seller at the close of a transaction involving the exchange of property for a specific consideration. The statement accounts for all funds received and expended by the escrow holder.

COBOL Acronym for Common Business Oriented Language. A specific language by which business data-processing procedures may be precisely described in a standard form.

cogeneration The generation of process steam, process heat, or space conditioning, combined with the generation of electric power, which leads to a greater efficiency of fuel utilization than that resulting from the independent generation of equivalent units of process steam, process heat, space conditioning, and electric power.

cognitive dissonance theory A type of perceptual bias which causes feelings of regret after an important purchase has been made as alternative opportunities that were considered seem to compare more favorably. Normally, the buyer will tend to resolve the tension by finding more advantages in support of his action and by downgrading the advantages of the rejected alternatives.

coincident indicators Time series that tend to move approximately in coincidence with the aggregate economy and are measures of current economic activity. *See* lagging indicators; leading indicators.

coinsurance An arrangement under which the insured shares in losses in the proportion that his insurance is less than a specified percentage of the value of the property insured; also an arrangement under which two or more insurers are each liable for a share of the losses.

cold storage warehouse A refrigerated warehouse that provides controlled low temperatures for the storage and preservation of perishable foods such as fruits and vegetables. Also used for storing furs, special chemicals, and other items requiring controlled low temperatures.

collateral Specific property which a borrower pledges as security for the repayment of a loan, agreeing that the lender has the right to sell the collateral for the purpose of liquidating the debt if the borrower fails to repay the loan at maturity. *See* security interest.

collective bargaining Workers, through a spokesman, bargain collectively rather than individually for wages and other issues.

collect on delivery (C.O.D.) This means that the purchaser is to receive the merchandise only if he pays for it on delivery.

collision insurance An automobile insurance coverage against damage to the policyholder's vehicle caused by collision with another car or object or by an upset.

combination advertising rate A special space rate granted in connection with two or more periodicals owned by the same publisher. Usually, the same space and copy must be used in each.

combination export manager An independent export firm that acts as the export sales department for more than one manufacturer. The combination export manager usually operates in its own name, but sometimes it operates in the name of a manufacturer-client for export markets. It may act as an independent distributor, purchasing and reselling goods at an established price or profit margin, or as a commission representative taking no title and bearing no final risks in the sale.

combination in restraint of trade An association of two or more individuals or corporations whose purpose is to monopolize the market for their product, or to fix its price, restrict its sale, or otherwise deal in unfair business practices.

commerce power The power given by the United States Constitution to the U.S. Congress in allowing it to control trade with foreign countries and trade between the states. *See* Interstate Commerce Act.

commercial The advertiser's message presented on a broadcast medium.

commercial blanket bond A fidelity bond to cover operators of commercial establishments against losses resulting from employees' dishonest acts.

commercial lines Insurance for businesses, organizations, institutions, governmental agencies, or other commercial establishments.

commercial loans Principally loans made to businesses for the financing of inventory purchases and the movement of goods, as distinguished from personal loans or consumer credit loans. Commercial loans are short-term loans or acceptances.

commercial multiple peril insurance A package type of insurance which includes a wide range of essential coverages for the commercial establishment.

commercial paper Short-term promissory notes issued and sold by corporations, municipalities, and public authorities, usually through dealers in such paper. These notes are negotiable instruments and usually carry a rating from the major credit-rating agencies.

commission broker An agent who executes the public's orders for the purchase or sale of securities or commodities.

commission merchant An agent, broker, or factor employed to sell goods, wares, and merchandise consigned or delivered to him by his principal for a compensation.

commissions Monies paid to an executor of an estate, agent, broker, trustee, or receiver for his or her services. Such monies are usually a percentage of the total amounts involved in the transaction or estate.

commitment An agreement, often in writing, between a lender and a borrower to loan money at a future date subject to compliance with stated conditions.

commitment fee A fee paid by a potential borrower to a potential lender for the latter's promise to lend money at a specified date in the future. The lender may or may not expect to fund the commitment. The interest rate may or may not be specified at the time the commitment fee is paid. *See* advance commitment.

Committee on Uniform Securities Identification Procedures (CUSIP) A universal securities-numbering system used by virtually all brokers and dealers executing transactions in the United States. The actual work of assigning numbers to securities is handled by Standard and Poor's CUSIP Service Bureau.

commodity Raw materials, semifinished goods, or economic goods in general which have established standards of quality, and which are traded in established quantities for spot delivery or for future delivery.

Commodity Credit Corporation A federal government agency whose function is to support prices of agricultural products through subsidies and the purchase of loans, and to help sell such products in the domestic and foreign markets.

Commodity Futures Trading Commission An independent agency that regulates commodity futures markets, which involves purchases and sales of contracts for certain quantities of specified commodities at fixed prices for delivery at some future date. The Commission's function is to bring under regulation all commodities traded on commodity exchanges; to prevent price manipulation and the dissemination of false or misleading information that might affect prices; to protect against cheating, fraud, and abusive practices in commodity transactions; and to safeguard the handling of traders' margin money and equities by preventing misuse of such funds by brokers.

commodity price adjustment clause A clause in an electric rate schedule that provides for an adjustment of the customer's bill if the price of commodities or index of commodity prices varies from a specified standard.

commodity rates A system of freight charges that takes into account the special characteristics of a particular commodity shipped between specified points, as related to volume and distance.

common carrier A person or corporation, licensed by an authorized state, federal, or other governmental agency, engaged in the business of transporting personal property from one place to another for compensation.

common cost Cost resulting from the use of a facility (e.g., plant or machines) or a service (e.g., fire insurance) that benefits several products or departments and must be allocated to those products or departments.

common stock Stock representing the class of owners who have residual claim on the assets of a corporation after all debts and preferred stockholders' claims have been met. *See* preferred stock.

company union An organization of employees of a single plant or company not affiliated with any national organization.

comparables An abbreviation for comparable properties used for comparative purposes in the appraisal process. Facilities of reasonably the same size and location with similar amenities. Properties which have characteristics similar to property under consideration, thereby indicating the approximate fair market value of the subject property.

comparison advertising Advertisements which directly compare one or more specific characteristics of the advertiser's product or brand with at least one competing brand that is named or made clearly recognizable.

compensating balance The amount of money required to be kept on deposit in a lending bank by a borrowing company as a condition for obtaining a loan. Such a requirement decreases the effective principal borrowed and increases the effective interest rate of a loan.

compensation Remuneration or payment for services rendered; also money paid to an injured employee.

competition A state of rivalry existing among several persons or business firms seeking the same or similar goods, rewards, or satisfactions.

competitive bidding A procedure in which bids are sent to several bidders, all of whom are treated equally and are bidding under similar terms. Usually, utility and municipal bonds are sold on a competitive bid basis. Contracts with government agencies are awarded in a similar way. *See* negotiated underwriting.

competitive stage The advertising stage a product reaches when its general usefulness is recognized but its superiority over similar brands has to be established in order to gain preference.

competitive state insurance fund A facility established by a state to write workers' compensation insurance in competition with private insurers.

competitive wage The wages which a company must pay its employees in order to be able to hold them or to recruit employees when needed in carrying out its production schedules.

compiler A special program that changes statements from one language into another, usually into machine language.

completed contract method Accounting for revenues and expenses for a job or order only when it is finished, except when a loss on the job or order is expected.

completion bond A bond furnished by a contractor to guarantee completion of construction.

compound interest Interest resulting from the periodic addition of simple interest to principal, the new base thus established being the principal used for the computation of interest for the next following interest period. *See* simple interest.

compound or mixed duties These duties provide for specific rates plus ad valorem rates to be levied on the same articles.

comprehensive personal liability insurance Protection for an insured against loss arising out of the policyholder's legal liability to pay money for damage or injury to others. Does not include automobile liability or business operations.

comptroller A city or state official who looks after monetary and fiscal affairs. His tasks include the examination and audit of accounts, the keeping of records, and the supervision of those who collect public money.

Comptroller General The head of the General Accounting Office, an arm of the legislative branch of the federal government. Reports directly to the U.S. Congress on the financial position and accounting systems of government agencies and, at the request of Congress, provides critiques related to agency organization and management. *See* General Accounting Office.

compulsory arbitration A system whereby the parties to a dispute are forced by the government to forgo their right to strike and are compelled to accept the resolution of their dispute through arbitration by a third party. Parties may also agree in advance to resolve disputes through compulsory arbitration.

compulsory insurance Any form of insurance which is required by law.

computer A data processor that can perform substantial computations, including numerous arithmetic or logic operations, without intervention by a human operator during the run.

computer console A set of switches and indicator lamps that allows the computer operator to control and monitor certain aspects of operation.

computer language The combination of words and phrases through which a person can give instructions to a computer.

computer program A series of instructions or statements, in a form acceptable to a computer, prepared in order to achieve a certain result.

concealment The withholding of material facts regarding the nature of an insurance risk or loss. Withholding essential information from the insurer in negotiating an insurance contract or in making a claim.

concentration campaign An advertising campaign concentrating on a market by using only pertinent media but advertising with great force in those outlets.

concentration ratio The percentage of an industry's output accounted for by several leading firms.

concentric diversification Refers to a company's seeking to add new products that have technological and/or marketing synergies with the existing product line; these products will normally appeal to new classes of customers.

conceptual skill The ability of a person to see the overall scope of issues and considerations relating to his and his associates' affairs.

conciliation A dispute settlement procedure in labor relations which uses a neutral third party to clarify the issues in a dispute so that the parties concerned may themselves arrive at a mutually acceptable agreement. *See* fact-finding board.

concurrent resolution of the budget A resolution passed by both houses of Congress, but not requiring the signature of the President, setting forth, reaffirming, or revising the congressional budget for the United States government for a fiscal year. There are two such resolutions required preceding each fiscal year. *See* reconciliation process.

condemnation Taking private property under the right of eminent domain for public use with compensation to the owner.

condensed balance sheet An abbreviated balance sheet which includes only major balance sheet accounts.

conditional commitment A commitment on a specific property for a definite loan amount with specific terms for some future unknown purchaser of satisfactory credit standing.

conditional contract A contract in which the performance depends on the fulfillment of a specified condition.

conditional sale lease A lease that in substance is a conditional sale. Sometimes called a hire-purchase agreement.

conditional sales agreement A contract that provides for the term financing of asset purchases. The seller retains title to the assets until all the conditions, such as installment payments, have been fulfilled. At that time, title is automatically vested in the purchaser.

condition precedent A condition that must exist prior to the conclusion of a contract or agreement.

condominium A form of ownership of real property. The purchaser receives title to a particular unit and a proportionate interest in certain common areas. A condominium generally defines each unit as a separately owned space surrounded by the interior surfaces of the perimeter walls, floors, and ceilings. Title to the common areas is in terms of percentages and refers to the entire project less the separately owned units.

confidence interval In statistics, a range of adjacent values used to estimate the true value of a parameter with a specified degree of probability; generally superior to "point estimates." The probability associated with a confidence interval is the "confidence level"; it is determined by choice and usually set at 95 percent, or 99.9 percent. The two end points of the interval are the "confidence limits."

confirmation The report of all relevant data sent by a broker to a client as a formal memorandum of any securities contract assumed by the client.

confirming bank A correspondent bank that adds its own guarantee to that of the issuing bank in a letter of credit transation, guaranteeing that the credit will be honored by the issuer or a third bank.

conglomerate A corporation composed of several subsidiary corporations, some of which may be engaged in business in completely different industries. These types of companies are usually formed by mergers or acquisitions of several companies.

conglomerate diversification Refers to a company's seeking to add new products that have no relationship to the company's current technology, products, or markets; these products will normally appeal to new classes of customers.

conglomerate integration Acquisition of one company by another in an unrelated business and not necessarily in the same channel of distribution.

congressional recission The consequence of enacted legislation which cancels budget authority previously provided by the U.S. Congress prior to the time when the authority would otherwise lapse.

connection charge An amount to be paid by an electric system customer in a lump sum, or in installments, for connecting the customer's facilities to the supplier's facilities.

consideration The inducement to a contract. The cause, motive, price, or impelling influence which induces a contracting party to enter into a contract.

consignee A person to whom a shipper directs a carrier to deliver goods, generally the buyer.

consignment Goods shipped for future sale or other purpose, while the title remains with the shipper, for which the receiver, upon his acceptance, is accountable.

consolidated financial statement A financial statement which includes the overall results of a corporation's many subsidiaries, with intersubsidiary transactions eliminated.

consolidated tape Under the Consolidated Tape Plan, the New York Stock Exchange and AMEX ticker systems became the "Consolidated Tape," Network A and Network B, respectively, on June 16, 1975. Network A reports transactions in New York Stock Exchange-listed securities which take place on the Exchange or on any of the participating regional stock exchanges and other markets. Each transaction is identified according to its originating market. Similarly, transactions in AMEX-listed securities, and certain other securities listed on regional stock exchanges, are reported and identified on Network B.

consortia bank A permanent group of banks whose objective is to provide joint financing to customers.

consortium banks Consortium banks are common in the Euromarket and are active in loan syndication and may be owned by or be affiliates of one or more banks.

construction contract An agreement between a general contractor and an owner-developer stating the specific duties the general contractor will perform according to blueprints and specifications at a stipulated price and terms of payment.

construction costs All costs incurred in bringing a building to completion, not including land-acquisition cost or finance sales and legal costs.

construction loan A short-term interim loan for financing the cost of construction. The lender makes payments to the builder at periodic intervals as the work progresses. Takeout commitment may or may not be in place. *See* development loan; mortgage.

construction loan agreement A written agreement between a lender and a builder/contractor in which the specific terms and conditions of a construction loan, including the schedule of payments, are specified.

construction loan draw The partial disbursement of the construction loan, based on the schedule of payments in the loan agreement. Also called takedown.

consumer advertising Directed at people who will personally use the product, in contrast to trade advertising, industrial advertising, professional advertising.

consumer behavior Results of actions of individuals involved in deciding which goods and services to purchase. The expectation of consumers vis-à-vis interest rates, inflation rates, and other economic factors influence the development of economic cycles.

consumer credit Credit extended by a bank to a borrower for the specific purpose of financing the purchase of a household appliance, alteration or improvement, or piece of equipment (which may include an automobile or small aircraft). This credit is generally extended to individuals rather than to businesses. The largest field for this type of financing is in household appliances and home improvements, such as insulation work, furnaces, and storm windows and doors. The loan is made for twelve, eighteen, twenty-four months, or longer, and a liquidation arrangement is usually based upon a definite repayment of equal monthly installments. *See* Truth in Lending Loans.

consumer goods Goods purchased and used by the consumer for his personal or household use.

consumerism An increasingly prominent activity by consumers and government to take the necessary measures to protect the general public from product misrepresentation, poorly made goods, bad service, and obscure warranties.

consumer markets The groups of individuals and households which buy products intended for personal consumption.

consumer price index A statistical measure of change in the prices of goods and services bought by urban wage earners and clerical workers (families and single persons living alone). It is calculated by comparing from one period to the next the cost of a market basket of goods and services usually purchased by this particular population group. *See* industrial production index.

Consumer Product Safety Act A 1972 act of Congress, its express purposes include protecting the public against unreasonable risks of injury associated with products, developing uniform safety standards, and promoting research and investigation into the causes and prevention of product-related injuries.

Consumer Product Safety Commission An independent regulatory agency whose purpose is to protect the consumer against unreasonable risks associated with consumer products. The Commission assists in evaluating the comparative safety of consumer products, develops uniform safety standards for such products, attempts to minimize conflicts between state and local regulations, and promotes research and investigation into product-related deaths, illnesses, or injuries.

containerization Shipment of large, sealed containers via rail, truck, or water to reduce transit time, pilferage, damage, packaging, and, at times, costs, through less frequent freight handling. *See* piggybacking.

contango Market situation in which prices are progressively higher in the future delivery months than in the nearest delivery month. *See* backwardation.

contingency management Management technique which recognizes differences or contingencies in people, at various times and in actual situations; also referred to as situational management. An approach that emphasizes there can be no one best way to solve various kinds of situations.

contingency planning Planning for possible future business conditions which are not expected to occur but which may occur. If this possible future is greatly different from that which is premised, alternative strategies are required.

contingent annuity An annuity whose number of payments depends upon the outcome of an event the timing of which is uncertain when the annuity is set up.

contingent fee system A method of paying for the services of a professional in which the client pays a certain sum, depending upon how much is earned. Said sum is usually a percentage of the monies collected, rather than a flat, fixed fee.

contingent liabilities Items which may become legal or financial liabilities as a result of conditions undetermined at a given date; for example, guarantees, standby letters of credit, pending law suits, judgments under appeal, unsettled disputed claims, unfilled purchase orders, and uncompleted contracts.

contingent rentals Rentals in which the amount depends on some factor other than the passage of time.

continuation strategy A marketing strategy in which the firm continues to use the same market segments, channels, pricing, and promotion.

continuing guaranty In freight movement, refers to the seals on a car or truck that remain intact during the movement of the car or truck from point of origin to destination.

continuing resolution Legislation enacted by the U.S. Congress to provide budget authority for specific ongoing activities in cases where the regular fiscal-year appropriation for such activities has not been enacted by the beginning of the fiscal year.

continuous production A production system in which the productive units are organized and sequenced according to the steps necessary to make the product. The routing of the jobs is fixed, and setups are seldom changed. The process of production may be around-the-clock. *See* intermittent production.

contra account An account, such as accumulated depreciation, that accumulates subtractions from another account, like equipment.

contract An agreement between two or more parties upon legal and sufficient consideration, obligating the parties to perform or refrain from performing specific actions. It represents the legal relationship that exists after an agreement has been reached. Contracts are of varying form (oral, written, implied at law, and others), and require varying degrees of formality and continue for an agreed period of time.

contract authority A form of budget authority under which contracts or other obligations may be entered into in advance of an appropriation or in excess of amounts otherwise available in a revolving fund. Contract authority must be funded by a subsequent appropriation or the use of revolving-fund collections to liquidate the obligations.

contract bond A guarantee of the faithful performance of a construction contract, and usually the payment of all labor and material bills related to it.

contract liability insurance Coverage for a loss for which the policyholder has assumed another's liability under contract.

contract of sale A legally binding contract between a purchaser and a seller of real property to convey a title after certain conditions have been met and payments have been made.

contract price The agreed amount of money to be paid under a contract to render a service or secure a product. Such price may be established in advance of the contract signing.

contractual obligation The binding obligation which arises from a contract or agreement.

contractual vertical marketing system A process through which independent firms at different levels of production and distribution integrate their programs on a contractual basis to obtain more economies of scale and sales impact compared with individual activity.

contributed capital The payments in cash or property made to a corporation by its stockholders in exchange for capital stock, in response to an assessment on the capital stock, or as a gift; also known as paid-in capital.

controllability in budgeting The ability under existing law to control budget authority or outlays during a given fiscal year.

controlled circulation publications Mailed without cost to people responsible for making buying decisions. Also known as qualified circulation publications.

controlled company A company that, vis-à-vis voting stock, is under the active control of a holding or a parent company.

controller The chief accountant of an organization responsible for financially related areas.

controlling The management function of monitoring that plans are carried out successfully in accordance with stated company policy guidelines.

control process In management-control systems, the basic process involves establishing standards, measuring performance against standards, and correcting for deviations.

convenience goods Consumer goods that the customer purchases frequently, and with a minimum of effort in comparison shopping and buying. Little advertising is associated with the sale of these goods.

convenience store This store is usually located far from major shopping centers and sells national brand-name merchandise at higher prices. *See* regional shopping center.

conversion The replacement of one class of corporate security with another class.

convertibility In foreign exchange, the ability to convert one currency into another.

convertible bond A bond that under the terms of the bond indenture may be exchanged, at the option of the holder and subject to specified limitations of time, rate of exchange, number of securities, and other conditions, for common stock or another security for the issuer. *See* convertible Euro-bond.

convertible Euro-bond A Euro-bond that can be converted into equity of the issuing company under prescribed conditions. *See* convertible bond.

convertible preferred stock Preferred stock that may be converted into a specified number of shares of common stock.

conveyance Refers to the transfer by mortgage, deeds, bill of sale, or other means, of title property from one party to another.

cooperative A form of multiple ownership of real estate in which a corporation or business trust entity holds title to a property and grants the occupancy rights to particular apartments or units to shareholders by means of proprietary leases or similar arrangements.

cooperative advertising Advertising of a product by a retailer, dealer, distributor, or similar party, with a portion of the advertising cost paid by the product's manufacturer.

cooperative association An organization composed of a group of individuals who have joined together for the achievement of a common goal for their mutual profit and purpose.

cooperative chain A group of retailers who form their own wholesaling enterprise in order to compete with corporate chains.

cooperative exporter An export organization of a United States manufacturing company retained by other independent manufacturers to sell their products in some or all foreign markets.

copyright The right of ownership in published or artistic property, under laws vesting the right in the creator of that property for specified times and extending it by international agreements to much of the world. The owner of a copyright often sells or leases rights in that property for publication or for television or the movies.

copyright abandonment Copyright which has not been obtained prior to publication.

copywriter A person who creates the text of advertisements and often the idea to be visualized or presented.

corporate planning A staff function on a senior corporate level which is responsible for long-range and strategic planning for the corporation. The implementation of these plans is usually a line function, and at times only a part of the plan may be implemented in a given time frame.

corporate reorganization An administrative or a legal reorganization for the purpose of strengthening the financial or market position of the corporation.

corporate resolution A document given to a bank by a corporation that defines the authority vested in each of its officers who may sign and otherwise conduct corporation business with the bank. Corporate resolutions are given with or without borrowing powers. These powers are granted by the board of directors of the firm.

corporate vertical marketing system Any vertically aligned group of firms which works as a unit to reduce the costs inherent in merchandising a line or classification of goods.

corporation A body of persons granted a charter by a state legally recognizing it as a separate entity having its own rights, privileges, and liabilities distinct from those of its members. *See* articles of incorporation.

correlation The relationship between two series of data, such as between two quantities, so that when one changes, the other is likely to make a corresponding change. If the changes are in the same direction, there is a positive correlation. When changes tend to go in opposite directions, there is negative correlation.

correspondent bank A bank which acts as a representative bank for one or more smaller banks. Could also be a domestic correspondent of a foreign bank.

cosigner Someone who signs a document along with another person, often assuming obligations and providing credit support to be shared with the other obligors.

cost An expenditure or outlay of cash, other property, capital stock, or services, or the incurring of a liability.

cost accounting A method of accounting which provides management with product cost information. It includes the collection, recording, allocation, and evaluation of such costs for the purpose of understanding, controlling, and projecting both individual product and total business expenses.

cost approach to value An approach to appraisal of the value of a property which derives the estimated replacement cost of the improvement and deducts therefrom the estimated depreciation, then adds the value of the land as estimated by use of the market data approach.

cost center In cost accounting, any department, process, machine, or other element of a firm for which cost records are maintained and to which fixed costs are allocated along with direct labor and material costs.

cost-effectiveness An approach to decision making which looks at alternatives and selects the one whose ratio of benefit to cost is the highest.

cost, insurance, freight, named port of destination In terms of sales, this indicates that the seller will pay all charges involved in getting goods to a destination.

cost method A way of accounting for an investment in another venture in which the investment is shown at acquisition cost, and only dividends received are treated as revenue.

cost of capital The weighted average cost of a company of its various sources of capital. Such costs may result from interest on debt, or from the dividends and capital growth realized by common stockholders. The cost of capital is normally used in determining the minimum return a company should accept on any new investment it undertakes.

cost of goods purchased Purchase price of goods acquired plus costs of storage, insurance, and delivery to the place where the items can be used.

cost of goods sold The cost of production of finished goods sold by the manufacturer.

cost of money The cost a borrower incurs to borrow money under his bank lines of credit. This includes the interest rate and any additional costs related to such borrowing, such as fees or compensating balances.

cost or market, whichever is lower Inventory valuation in which the cost is set at the lowest of the following: acquisition cost, current replacement cost, or market value.

cost overrun Funds required or expended over and above budget costs, including such items as labor, materials, and additional financing.

cost per thousand Refers to readers, viewers, and circulation. Used in comparing the costs of alternative vehicles of advertising.

cost-plus A contract in which the purchaser agrees to pay the vendor an amount determined by the costs incurred by the vendor to produce the goods and/or services purchased, and to whose profits are added a stated percentage or fixed sum.

countersign The signature of a secretary or other subordinate officer of a corporation authorized by the principal or superior to vouch for the authenticity of the original signature.

coupon rate The interest rate established at the time of issuance of a bond issue. The coupon rate is the annual interest paid, expressed as a percentage of the bond's face value. If the bond is selling at a price other than its face value, its yield will not equal its coupon rate.

covenant A legally enforceable promise or restriction in the terms of a corporate debt instrument, mortgage, or contract. Such a constraint might require a company to maintain certain compensating balances or not to exceed specified financial ratios while a loan is outstanding.

covenant to convey A covenant by which the covenantor agrees to convey to the covenantee a certain estate under certain conditions.

covenant to renew A clause in a contract giving a person (the one leasing the property) the right to renew the terms of the contract under certain conditions outlined in the prior contract.

coverage ratio The ratio of income available to pay a specific obligation, net of the income required to pay senior debt, if any, to the total amount obligated. It is a measure of a firm's ability to service specific obligations such as interest charges, preferred stock, and common stock dividends. *See* debt service.

covered interest arbitrage A process of borrowing a currency, converting it into another currency where it is invested at the local interest rate, and selling this other currency for future delivery against the initial currency. The profits in this transaction are derived from discrepancies between interest differentials and the percentage discounts or premiums among the currencies involved in the transaction.

covering Generally refers to trade transactions that produce a payable or a receivable account in foreign exchange to be liquidated at a future date. The covering transaction eliminates the risk of fluctuations in foreign exchange rates during the intervening period. Covering and hedging are terms that are often used interchangeably.

craft unions Unions comprised mainly of skilled craft workers, such as machinists and electricians. *See* industrial unions.

credit The ability of a person or business to borrow money or obtain goods on time because of a lender's acceptable view as to solvency and reliability.

credit analysis A financial and management review conducted by a lender or a credit-rating agency to determine the fiscal soundness and debt-repayment ability of a corporation, municipality, foreign government, or an individual. *See* bond rating.

credit file A portfolio in which all public and bank information on a customer is assembled. Financial statements, records of indebtedness, law suits, court actions, credit references, various credit reports, call memoranda, important correspondence, and credit-department analyses are deposited in this portfolio or file.

credit insurance A guarantee to manufacturers, wholesalers, and service organizations that they will be paid for goods shipped or services rendered. It is a guarantee of that part of their working capital represented by accounts receivable.

creditor An individual to whom a debt is owed.

credit rating A rating given a person or company that reflects credit worthiness and ability to pay back debt based upon present financial condition, experience, past credit history, and other factors.

credit report A report to a prospective lender secured from a credit bureau on the credit condition of a prospective borrower, used to help determine credit standing.

credit tranche The amount of funds that a member country of the International Monetary Fund can borrow from the Fund.

credit union A nonprofit corporation whose purpose is to promote savings and to make small loans to members. A credit union may be federally incorporated and is audited by the Federal Deposit Insurance Corporation.

critical path method A network planning technique used for preparing and controlling the activities in a project. By showing each of these activities and their associated times, the "critical path" can be determined. The critical path identifies those elements that actually limit the total time for the project. *See* program evaluation and review technique (PERT).

crop-hail insurance Insurance protection against damage to growing crops as a result of hail or certain other perils.

cross rate The calculation of a foreign exchange rate from two separate quotes that contain the same currency.

cumulative dividend Preferred stock dividends which, if not paid, accrue as an obligation that must be paid before dividends to common stockholders can be declared.

cumulative markup This represents in dollars and percent the markup obtained by a buyer or merchant on an accumulated group of similar merchandise which has been purchased and sold.

current account In the balance of payments, the section that records the trade in goods and services and the exchange of gifts among countries.

current asset An asset whose future benefit will occur within a short period, usually one year. Current assets include cash, marketable securities, receivables, inventory, and current prepayments.

current income Income earned within the current year or current accounting period and not from income generated as a result of activities over many accounting periods. *See* deferred compensation.

current liability A debt that must be discharged within a short time, usually one year.

current ratio A measure of a company's liquidity, obtained by dividing current assets by current liabilities. *See* acid test ratio; quick ratio.

current value The current value of imported commodities is their common market price at the place of export.

customer charge An amount to be paid periodically by an electric system customer without regard to demand or energy consumption.

customer profile A projection of the demographic characteristics of the people who buy a brand and the purchase patterns they will produce.

customs Duties payable on imported merchandise, levied according to existing customs laws.

customs court A federal court responsible for reviewing levies made by customs collectors and for acting upon complaints from importers of goods and materials.

cybernetics A branch of technology and science which brings together theories and studies on communication and control in living organisms and machines.

cyclical fluctuations Variations in business and industrial output with successive periods of positive and negative percent deviations around the secular trend curve of a time series, with the duration of a complete cycle of fluctuation being more than one year.

D

damages Compensation which may be recovered through legal action by any person who has suffered loss or injury, whether to his person, property, or rights, through the unlawful act, omission, or negligence of another.

data A collection of facts, concepts, or instructions in a formalized manner suitable for communication, interpretation, or processing by humans or by automatic methods.

data bank A comprehensive collection of libraries of data.

data base A collection of data fundamental to calculations used for scientific or management purposes.

data base management A set of rules about file organization and processing, generally contained in complex software, which controls the definition and access of complex, interrelated files which are shared by numerous application systems.

data file A collection of related data records organized in a specific manner which can be accessed through the computer.

data management An operating system function that involves organizing, cataloging, locating, storing, retrieving, and maintaining data.

data-processing system A network of machine components capable of accepting information, processing it according to a plan, and producing the desired results.

data reduction The formal approach of transforming masses of data into useful, ordered, or simplified intelligence.

date of invoice—ordinary dating In transportation, the discount period for the prepayment begins with the date of the invoice. The net amount is also due within the specified time from the date of the invoice.

dead time Periods when an employee is prevented from continuing his work because of factors beyond his control, such as material or power shortages, mechanical breakdowns, or other unavoidable delays.

deal An arrangement or transaction entered into to attain a desired result by interested parties, the prime object being usually the purchase, sale, or exchange of property or service for a profit.

dealer tie-in Participation by a dealer in a national advertiser's promotional program.

debenture A certificate of indebtedness of a company which is not secured by any specific asset but which is backed by its general credit.

debit An accounting designation for the left-hand side of an account.

debt An oral or a written obligation to pay an amount incurred in exchange for money, goods, or services, and usually carrying a specified maturity and interest rate. Debt may take many forms, such as a note, bond, or debenture, and be for a short, intermediate, or long-term period.

debt capacity The amount of debt a company can issue before the cost of financing becomes prohibitively high. As a company increases the amount or percentage of debt in its capital structure, its ability to repay the principal and interest when due becomes less assured.

debt coverage ratio The ratio of effective annual net income to annual debt service.

debtor One who owes a debt and is liable by contract to pay a claim for repayment of money owed.

debt participant A long-term lender in a financial transaction, who may be represented by one or more financial institutions. *See* equity participant.

debt ratio Long-term debt in various forms, divided by the total amount of a company's capital. The debt ratio is a measure of a company's financial leverage.

debt service The periodic payment of principal and interest earned on a debt instrument. *See* coverage ratio.

debug To detect, locate, and remove mistakes from a routine or malfunctions from a computer, a manufacturing process, or a control system.

decentralization Decision making and administrative controls delegated to the lowest possible levels of the organization. *See* centralization.

decentralization of authority A management approach which disperses decision-making authority in an organizational structure. *See* centralization of authority.

decision formulation The process of determining further courses of action based on the interrelationship among the available choices, their relative importance, and in accordance with established parameters.

decision making The selection from among various options of a course of action that will most likely lead to the benefits, profits, or outcomes sought.

decision tree A method of analysis that uses a graphic technique to evaluate alternative decisions in a treelike structure to estimate values and probabilities of outcomes. The expected likelihood of each outcome is the sum of all similar outcomes and their chance of occurring.

declaration The part of a property or liability insurance policy which includes such information as the name and address of the insured, the property insured, its location and description, the policy period, the amount of coverage, applicable premiums, and supplemental information provided by the insured.

declaration of dividend The act of a corporation in setting aside a portion of the net or surplus proceeds for distribution among the stockholders according to the shares they own.

declared valuation In transportation, the valuation placed on a shipment when it is delivered to the carrier.

declining balance A technique of accelerated depreciation which establishes as much as twice the straight-line method of depreciation without regard to salvage value.

deductible An amount which a policyholder agrees to pay, per claim or per accident, toward the total amount of an insured loss. Insurance is written on this basis at reduced rates.

deductible expenses Expenditures allowed for business purposes that can be deducted from the income taxes of the person or corporation.

deed A written document by which the ownership of real property is transferred from one party to another.

deed in lieu A deed given by a mortgagor to a mortgagee to satisfy a debt and without going through the process of foreclosure.

deed of reconveyance The transfer of legal title from the trustee to the borrower after the trust deed debt is paid in full.

deed of trust A conveyance of the title land to a trustee as collateral security for the payment of debt with the requirement that the trustee reconvey the title upon the payment of the debt.

default The failure to pay interest or principal on a debt when due or to perform other requirements of a contract. *See* insolvency.

defeasance clause A clause in a contract which provides that performance of certain specified acts will render a contract void.

deferred asset An asset purchased in advance of the actual consumption of its benefits.

deferred charge An expenditure not recognized as an expense of the period when made, but carried forward to be written off in future periods.

deferred compensation A payment that a corporation is committed to make to an executive at some future date in the form of a deferred bonus, percentage of salary, or other payments. *See* current income.

deferred income tax The estimated income tax on the excess of net revenues, recognized for accounting purposes, over that reported for tax purposes.

deferred interest mortgage (DIM) A type of graduated payment mortgage with low initial payments over a period of years as if it were based on a lower interest rate than that on a standard fixed payment mortgage. Negative amortization accrues and is paid off with higher payments later.

deficiency judgment A court order to pay the balance owed on a loan if the proceeds from the sale of the collateral are insufficient to pay off the loan and satisfy the loan agreement.

deficit The excess of the liabilities and reserves of a fund over its assets.

deficit financing The governmental practice of deliberately budgeting expenditures in excess of actual or expected revenues.

delegation The authority given to an individual by his superior to complete the work assigned to him.

delinquency ratio The ratio of past-due loans to total loans serviced in the portfolio.

delinquent A debt that is due and has not been paid on a timely basis.

delivered duty paid Under this contract, the seller undertakes to deliver the goods to the buyer at the place he names in the country of import with all costs paid, including duties.

delivery In mortgage finance, the legal, final, and irrevocable transfer of a deed from seller to buyer in such a manner that it cannot be recalled by the seller.

delivery period The length of time which elapses from the time the order is placed until the goods are received into stock and ready for marketing.

demand The quantity of goods or services that will be purchased at a given price. *See* supply.

demand charge The specified charge to be billed on the basis of the billing demand, under an applicable rate schedule or contract.

demand deposit A bank deposit such as in a passbook or checking account which is payable to its depositor upon demand.

demand forecast The anticipation of future sales volume and trends.

demand note A note which states that it is payable on demand, on presentation, or at sight.

demographic characteristics The statistics of an area's population or market, delineating distinguishing characteristics such as age, sex, income, education, marital status, and occupation.

demotion The downward movement to a job of lesser responsibility and pay.

density zoning A zoning ordinance relating to subdivisions which restricts the number of houses that can be built per acre in a development.

department A distinct area, division, or branch of a business or governmental agency over which a manager has authority for the performance of specified activities and results.

department store A store which is a collection of specialty stores under one roof.

depletion allowance A bookkeeping entry represented by charges against earnings, based upon the amount of the asset taken out of the total reserves in the period for which the accounting is made.

depletion deduction An income tax deduction granted for use of mineral deposits and other resources, such as oil and gas, or a forest whose trees are used through commercial means.

depreciable cost That part of the cost of an asset which is to be charged over the life of the asset, usually the cost less the estimated recovery from resale or salvage.

depreciable life The estimated period of time over which a capital asset can be depreciated under established tax laws and regulations.

depreciation The reduction in an asset's value through wear, tear, or obsolescence, and is the business expense which is recognized due to the expiration of a capital asset's usefulness. It is solely a bookkeeping entry and, as such, is a noncash charge against income. *See* allowance for depreciation.

depreciation allowance A charge permitted to be deducted annually as an expense, resulting in a decrease in adjusted basis.

depth interview An interview conducted without a structured questionnaire. Respondents are encouraged to speak fully and freely about a particular subject area.

designated market area A region in which originating stations have a greater share of the viewing or listening households than those from any other area.

devaluation A governmental action that makes a domestic currency cheaper in terms of other currencies. The action is taken to increase a nation's exports while reducing imports.

developer A person or entity who prepares parcels of land for building sites, and sometimes organizes contractors and others for the building of a specific structure. *See* front-end money.

development loan A short-term loan made for the purpose of preparing raw land for the construction of buildings. Development process may include grading and the installation of utilities and roadways and other infrastructure items. *See* construction loan.

development rights Rights sold by landowners to a developer or builder for developing and improving the property.

differentiation A characteristic of an open socioeconomic system, by which it tends to become more specialized in its structure, job patterns, and behavior.

dilution A potential reduction in earnings per share caused by the exercise of the convertible feature of securities or by the exercise of warrants or options.

direct control The assignment of high-quality managers to local premises in order to avoid errors and mistakes which, if they occur, may turn out to be very difficult to remedy.

direct costing The method of allocating costs that assigns only variable costs to products and treats fixed costs as period expenses.

direct costs Variable costs which can be directly attributed to a particular job, operation, or process. *See* indirect costs.

direct expenses Expenses which are charged directly as a part of the cost of a product, service, or department in contrast to overhead and indirect costs.

direct-financing lease A nonleveraged lease by a lessor in which the criteria of a capital lease are usually met.

direct foreign investment The purchase of a foreign financial asset in which substantial involvement in the management of the foreign operation is presumed, and usually requires an equity holding that represents more than 10 percent ownership of the foreign firm.

directing The management responsibility dealing with the close supervision of employees.

direct ıabor The cost of labor directly expended in the production of specific goods and services. *See* indirect labor.

direct-mail advertising Advertising which asks for an order to be sent by mail, and the delivery of the order is by mail.

direct marketing Selling goods and services without using a wholesaler or retailer. Uses many media—direct mail, publications, television, and radio.

direct materials The cost of materials that become part of the production of goods or rendition of services.

directors' and officers' liability insurance Coverage for directors and officers of firms or organizations against liability claims arising out of alleged errors in judgment, breaches of duty, and wrongful acts related to their business activities.

directory trust A trust where funds are vested in a specified manner.

direct-response advertising Advertising done via direct mail, television, magazines, newspapers, and radio.

direct writer An insurer whose distribution mechanism is either the direct-selling system or the exclusive agency system.

disability insurance An insurance policy usually run by a state government which will pay workers who are absent from work because of illness or injury.

disclosure An obligation to produce or make known information in one's possession; usually required in documents concerning the issuance/transfer of securities and in the presentation of financial statements.

discount The difference between face or future worth or value and present value of a payment. A reduction in price granted for the prompt payment of a debt. The rate of discount depends on money market conditions, credit rating of the financial instrument, and other factors. *See* par.

discount bond A bond selling below par. *See* premium bond.

discounted cash-flow analysis The process of determining the present value of future cash flows, assuming various interest rates.

discounting commercial paper The deduction of interest on a loan before the loan is made.

discount rate The rate of interest charged by Federal Reserve banks to member banks which borrow at the discount window.

discount securities Non-interest-bearing money market instruments that are issued at a discount and are redeemed at maturity for full face value, such as U.S. Treasury bills.

discount window A facility provided by the Federal Reserve System enabling member banks to borrow reserves against collateral in the form of government securities or other acceptable collateral.

discretionary income The amount of money a person has left after paying for basic food, clothing, shelter, insurance, taxes, and other necessities.

discretionary trust In a discretionary trust, no direction is given to the trustee as to precisely how the funds are to be invested or decisions taken.

disintermediation The flow of funds out of savings institutions into short-term investments, for example, through the use of money market funds, whose interest rates are higher. This shift normally results in a net decrease in the amount of funds available for long-term financing, such as bond issues.

disk rack A computer data-storage device. It rotates at high speed and can contain large (300 million characters) quantities of data stored magnetically on circular tracks.

display An attention-attracting visual presentation used in promotion.

display advertising In a newspaper, advertisements other than those in classified columns.

disposable personal income Money left over after taxes, union dues, and pension contributions are paid.

dispute A controversy between an employer and a union, or between unions, or between a union and its members, which usually leads to a strike or arbitration. *See* arbitration; strike.

dissipation of funds The reckless squandering of funds by a person in debt without regard to his obligations to his creditors.

distributed processing Data-processing approach when the computer resources of a company are installed at more than one location and are connected with appropriate communication links.

distribution The marketing and transporting of finished and semifinished products.

distribution channel The course the title to goods takes as it moves from producer to consumer through middlemen.

distribution of capital Corporate assets are distributed to the stockholders without paying the claims of the creditors or the corporation.

distributor A business selling manufactured products either to retail outlets (dealers) or directly to consumers. A distributor thus is identical to a wholesaler. *See* wholesaling.

diversification The investment of money, materials, and other resources in a variety of ways in order to limit the risk involved in the default of any one investment.

divestiture A corporation that sells one of its units to another firm is in the process of undertaking a divestiture.

dividend A distribution of a corporation's earnings paid to the owners of that corporation which may be paid in cash or with stock or other securities.

divisible contract A legal contract having several parts and for which remedy for nonperformance can be sought only for that part of the contract which has not been fulfilled. *See* indivisible contract.

documentation The process of collecting and organizing documents, or the information recorded in documents, in the form of materials specifying inputs, operations, and outputs of a computer system.

document of title Includes the bill of lading, dock warrant, dock receipt, warehouse receipt, and order for the delivery of goods; it serves as evidence that the person in possession of it is entitled to receive, hold, and dispose of the document and the goods it covers.

documents against acceptance In shipping, documents which are turned over to the importer upon his acceptance of a time draft on him.

documents against payment In shipping, documents which are turned over to the importer against payment of a sight draft for the amount payable to him by the exporter.

dollar (or foreign currency) drafts covering exports The draft may be on a sight basis for immediate payment, or it may be drawn to be accepted for payment for a specific period.

domestic corporation A corporate entity that is created under the laws of a given state or country in which the corporation is officially located.

domestic insurance company An insurer formed under the laws of the state in which the insurance is written.

double-declining-balance depreciation Declining-balance depreciation where the constant percentage is 2/n, in which n is the depreciable life in periods (n is greater than 2).

double entry A system of bookkeeping which requires that for every entry made on the debit side of an account, an entry for a corresponding amount be made on the credit side of another account.

double-page spread Facing pages used for a single, unbroken advertisement.

double taxation Taxing same item or property twice to the same person, or taxing it as the property of one person and again as the property of another.

Dow Jones Average Index of stock prices composed of four different averages of stocks.

Dow-Jones Industrial Average (DJIA) A quantitative measure of the performance of the stocks of thirty corporations listed on the New York Stock Exchange. The stocks that are measured are blue-chip stocks which at times behave differently from the norm. The index is used as a barometer of the performance, rise, and decline of the stock market.

down payment In mortgage finance, the difference between the sale price of real estate and the mortgage amount.

down tick In the stock market, a transaction made at the same price as the preceding sale but lower than the preceding different price. Indicated at each trading post on the floor of the New York Stock Exchange by a minus sign next to the last price of the stock traded.

downtime Time when the machines in the plant are not producing because they are down for repairs or other reasons. Also, when computers do not operate due to malfunction.

Dow Theory A theory of stock-market analysis based on the performance of certain stock-price averages. According to the theory, the market is in a basic upward trend if one of these averages advances beyond a previous important high and is accompanied or followed by a similar advance in another average. When both averages dip below important lows, this is regarded as confirmation of a downward trend.

dual-purpose fund A closed-end investment company that sells income shares and capital shares. Owners of income shares receive all the income the company obtains through dividend and interest payments. Owners of capital shares receive the profits the company obtains from capital gains.

due bill An instrument evidencing the obligation of a seller to deliver securities sold to another party.

dummy corporation A company organized as a legitimate legal enterprise but, in actuality, having the real corporate purpose of protecting certain parties against liability.

dump energy Energy which is generated in hydroelectric plants by water that cannot be stored or conserved and which is in excess of the needs of the electric system producing the energy.

dumping The sale of a product at a price below that normally charged in a domestic market or country of origin.

durable goods Tangible goods which can be expected to last for a relatively long time even though used repeatedly. *See* nondurable goods.

duress An action taken under pressure, coercion, or protest.

dutch auction A technique used in selling U.S. Treasury securities, in which the lowest price necessary to sell the entire offering becomes the price at which all securities offered are sold.

duty A tax levied by a government on the importation, exportation, or use and consumption of goods.

dynamic programming In operations research and management sciences, a procedure for optimization of a multistage problem solution in which a number of decisions are available at each stage of the process. *See* linear programming.

E

earned income Monies earned through one's labor, services, or work as distinguished from monies earned through interest or investments, ownership of property, or other capital gains.

earned premium The portion of a premium which is the property of an insurance company, based on the expired portion of the policy period.

earnings before interest and taxes The earnings that remain after all expenses are paid except interest and taxes.

earnings per share The net income for a stated period common stockholders receive, divided by the number of common shares outstanding.

easement A right of the owner of one parcel of land, by reason of such ownership, to use the land of another for a valid reason.

economic life The period of actual usefulness or profitability of an asset. Economic life refers to the period beyond which it is cheaper to replace or scrap an asset than to continue maintaining it.

economic order quantity A manufacturer's determination of the amount of product to be purchased or produced at one time in order to minimize the total cost involved, including the ordering and carrying expenses.

The Economic Recovery Tax Act of 1981 One of the cornerstones of Reaganomics. The Act liberalized the tax laws with respect to a variety of institutions and investment activities. It created business tax incentives, put in place income tax reductions, established tax exclusions on savings certificates, increased the limits for retirement contributions, and reduced the tax burden on gifts and exchanges.

economic rent The rent that a property would bring if offered in the open market as differentiated from the contract rent.

economic value The valuation of real property based on its earning capabilities.

economy energy Electric energy produced from a source in one system and substituted for energy that could have been produced by a less economical source in another system.

Edge Act Corporation A financial subsidiary of a United States bank set up to carry out international business. Most such subsidiaries are located within the United States in major money market centers.

effective annual interest rate The total amount, expressed as a percentage, which one dollar will earn in one year.

effective interest method An amortization method for a bond premium or discount that makes the interest expense for each period, divided by the amount of the net liability (face amount less discount or plus premium) at the beginning of the period, equal to the yield rate on the bond at the time of issue.

effective rate The real as distinct from the quoted yield on investments, calculating the yield as a percentage of market value rather than as a percentage of face value.

efficiency Maximum output with minimum inputs of labor capital and other resources.

elasticity A statistical measure of the degree to which a change in the quantity of an item demanded or supplied is impacted by a change in the price of the item.

electric generation The act or process of producing electric energy from other forms of energy; also, the amount of electric energy so produced.

electric rate The unit prices and the quantities to which they apply as specified in an electric rate schedule or sales contract.

electric system Physically connected electric generating, transmission, and distribution facilities operated as a unit under one control.

electronic data processing Data-processing equipment that is predominately electronic, for example, an electronic digital computer.

embargo A policy which prevents goods from entering a nation; may be imposed on a product or on an individual country.

embezzlement A fraudulent appropriation of money or property which is considered a criminal offense. *See* kickback.

eminent domain The right of a government to take private property for public use upon payment of its fair value. It is the basis for condemnation proceedings.

emotional buying motive A person's decision to buy that involves little or no thought.

employee association A union whose membership is made up almost entirely of professional, state, and local government workers.

employee discounts Special discounts, usually 10 percent to 25 percent, offered by retail establishments and other employers to specific employees.

Employee Retirement Income Security Act The Act's purpose is to protect the interests of workers and their beneficiaries who depend on benefits from employee pension and welfare plans. The law requires the disclosure of plan provisions and financial information; establishes standards of conduct for trustees and administrators of welfare and pension plans; sets up funding, participation, and vesting requirements for pension plans; and makes termination insurance available for most plans. It also provides that an employee not covered by a pension plan (other than Social Security) may put aside a certain amount of his income for retirement needs, the money remaining tax exempt until received as retirement benefits.

employee stock ownership plan A plan designed to give workers a sense of participation in the management of a company through the buying of stocks at specific prices.

employers' association A combination of employers of different firms to present united efforts in dealing with labor union demands.

employers' liability coverage A section of the workers' compensation policy which provides coverage against the common-law liability of an employer for injuries to employees as distinguished from the liability imposed by a workers' compensation law.

encroachment An improvement that intrudes illegally upon another's property.

encumbrance A lien or claim that affects or limits the fee simple title to property, such as mortgages, leases, easements, or restrictions.

end-of-month invoice Indicates that the invoice is to be paid within the designated number of days after the end of the month in which the goods were shipped.

endorsement A writing on a negotiable instrument by which title to property is assigned and transferred. A notation added to a legal instrument after its execution to change or clarify its contents. In insurance, the provisions may be restricted or enlarged by endorsing a policy.

endowment fund A fund whose principal and other investments must be maintained inviolate, but whose income may be expended for specific purposes.

end product advertising Advertising by a firm that refers to a constituent part of a finished product bought by the consumer. Also known as subordinate product advertising.

energy charge That portion of the billed charge for electric service which is based upon the electric energy (kilowatt-hours) supplied, as contrasted with the demand charge.

energy demand The rate at which electric energy is delivered to or by a system, part of a system, or piece of equipment, expressed in kilowatts or another suitable unit, at a given instant or averaged over any designated period of time.

energy distribution system That portion of an electric system used to deliver electric energy from points on the transmission or bulk power system to the consumers.

enterprise A project; an organization; a business venture; an undertaking.

enterprise fund A fund established to finance and account for the acquisition, operation, and maintenance of governmental facilities and services which are entirely or predominantly self-supporting by user charges. Examples of enterprise funds are those for water, gas, and electric utilities, swimming pools, airports, parking garages, and transit systems.

entitlement authority Legislation that requires the payment of benefits to any person or government meeting the requirements established by such law.

entity A person, partnership, corporation, or other organization engaged in business or legal activity.

entrepreneur The person, group, or organization which brings together the other factors in production so as to provide goods or services within acceptable risk and time elements. The entrepreneur may also have a substantial investment in the enterprise, but he contributes more than just capital. He may be responsible for initiating, planning, and providing managerial know-how to the functioning of the enterprise. Also known as a producer.

entry A record of facts and circumstances of a sale, trade, loan, or other transaction.

entry book A ledger of the registry of titles kept by the recorder of deeds.

environmentalism An organized social movement seeking to minimize the harm done by industrial practices to the environment and quality of life.

equipment-trust certificate An interest-bearing document marketed through private placement or public underwriting and evidencing a part of the ownership of a trust created for purchasing equipment and selling or leasing it to a user.

equity The net worth of a business, found by subtracting liabilities from assets.

equity capital Money supplied by the owners of a company in return for common stock or other evidence of ownership and share of profits. *See* capitalize.

equity of redemption The common-law right to redeem property during the foreclosure period. In some states the mortgagor has a statutory right to redeem property after a foreclosure sale. *See* redemption period.

equity participant The equity investor or owner in a leverage lease. Frequently a leverage lease transaction has more than one equity participant. *See* debt participant.

equivalent bond yield Annual yield on a short-term, non-interest-bearing security calculated so as to be comparable to yields quoted on coupon-bearing instruments.

equivalent taxable yield The yield on a taxable security that would provide the investor with the same after-tax return he would earn by holding a tax-exempt municipal security.

ergonomics The aspect of technology that is concerned with the application of biological and engineering data to problems relating to human beings and machines.

error Any discrepancy between a computed, observed, or measured quantity and the true, specified, or theoretically correct value or condition.

errors and omissions insurance A form of insurance that indemnifies the insured for any loss sustained because of an error or oversight on the part of the insured.

escalation clause An amount or percentage by which a contract price may be adjusted if specified contingencies occur, such as changes in the vendor's raw material, labor costs, and taxes.

escape clause A clause in a contract which allows under certain conditions a release or waiver of obligations specified in the contract.

escrow A contract, deed, or bond deposited with a third party, who holds such a legal instrument for the benefit of another until specific obligations are met by the obligor.

escrow account The segregated trust account in which escrow funds are held by an escrow agent.

escrow agent An entity having a fiduciary responsibility to both the buyer and seller (or lender and borrower) to see that the terms of the purchase/sale (or loan) are carried out.

escrow contract A three-party agreement of the buyer, seller, and escrow holder specifying the rights and duties of each.

estate The ownership interest that an individual has in real property. Also, the sum total of all the real and personal property owned by an individual at the time of death.

estate tax An excise tax on the privilege of transferring or transmitting property by reason of death; it is not a tax on property itself.

estimated tax An income tax that is based upon expected earnings, not upon income that has already been earned. Estimated taxes are usually paid in installments during the year.

estoppel letter A statement that in itself prevents its issuer from later asserting different facts.

ethical advertising Advertising that meets standards for fair, equitable, and honest content.

Euro-bond A bond denominated in the borrower's currency but sold outside the country of the borrower, usually by an international syndicate of banks and investment banks.

Euro-certificate of deposits Certificates issued by a United States bank branch or a foreign bank located outside the United States. Most of these instruments are issued in London.

Euro-currency Monies traded outside the countries in which they are the domestic currencies.

Euro-currency deposits Currencies held on deposit in banks in other countries and used as sources of financing by a wide variety of borrowers throughout the world.

Euro-dollars Dollar balances on deposit in banks outside the United States, including foreign branches of United States banks.

Euro-lines Lines of credit granted by banks (foreign or foreign branches of United States banks) in Euro-currencies.

eviction The legal removal of an occupant from real property.

evoked set The particular set of brands to which a consumer will limit his or her consideration of selection for purchase.

excess limits Coverage against losses in excess of a specified dollar limit.

excess reserves The amount of funds held by banks in reserve in excess of the legal minimum requirements.

exchange A specific marketplace in which instruments of ownership, such as stocks, bonds, and other valuables, are bought, sold, and traded.

exchange rate The price of one currency expressed in terms of another currency.

excise tax A tax on the manufacture, sale, or consumption of a commodity. Also known as a license tax or privilege tax.

exclusion A provision in an insurance policy which denies coverage for certain perils, persons, property, or locations.

exclusionary clause Contractual covenant which restricts the actions that a party can take if the other person fails to fulfill the provisions of the contract.

exclusive contract A business arrangement under which a person or corporation has sold the right to the trade, distribution, or purchasing of a commodity or service.

exclusive distribution When one dealer in a market area is given the right to distribute a product or service.

exculpatory clause A clause in a contract holding one party harmless in the event of some default.

ex-dividend A synonym for "without dividend." The buyer of a stock selling ex-dividend does not receive the recently declared dividend. Every dividend is payable on a fixed date to all shareholders recorded on the books of the company as a previous date of record. For example, a dividend may be declared as payable to holders of record on the books of the company on a given Friday. Since five business days are allowed for delivery of stock in a "regular-way" transaction on the New York Stock Exchange, the Exchange would declare the stock "ex-dividend" as of the opening of the market on the preceding Monday. That means anyone who bought it on and after Monday would not be entitled to that dividend. When stocks go ex-dividend, the stock tables include the symbol "x" following the name.

ex dock The seller's price quotation includes all costs necessary to place the goods on the dock of the named port of importation.

execute To complete or finish, or, in real estate deeds, to sign, seal, and deliver.

executed trust A trust for which all documentations and other requirements have been declared at the time the trust was formed.

execution sale A sale which is final and complete in all its particulars and details.

executive Member of an organization who is responsible for the performance of a total organization or of important segments of its activities.

executor A person named in a will to administer an estate. The courts appoint an administrator if no executor is named in a will.

exempt income Investment income which is exempt from federal or state taxation; for example, municipal bonds.

exemption Freedom from taxation, service duty, burden, or charge.

exempt property Real estate that is not subject to property taxation. Religious, educational and charitable organizations, and government agencies generally hold exempt property.

exempt securities Securities exempt from the registration requirements of the Securities and Exchange Act of 1934. Such securities include those of governments and agencies, municipal securities, commercial paper, and private placements. Municipal securities are issued under state and local legal requirements. *See* municipal bond.

exercise price The price per share at which stock may be purchased if the option is exercised; also called strike price.

exercising an option The right of first choice of buying something granted for a specific person for a period of time.

ex-factory When the seller is obligated to place the goods at the buyer's disposal at the point of origin; the seller must, however, still assist the buyer in obtaining any documents the latter may need for exporting and/or importing the goods.

exit interview A meeting between an employee who is leaving a company and a representative of the employer for the purpose of debriefing the employee on the causes of his leaving.

expectations-performance theory A consumer's satisfaction is a function of his product expectations and the product's perceived performance.

expedite To hasten to implement an action along prescribed directions.

expenditure Incurring a liability, transferring property, or paying cash to secure a product or service.

expense account Any account maintained for a particular expense.

expenses Charges incurred, whether paid or unpaid, for operation, maintenance, interest, and other charges, which are presumed to be accounted for in the current fiscal year.

experience rating An insurance company practice of charging different rates in the same policy depending on the perceived credit risk of the insured.

expert broker The expert broker, usually specializing in a product, receives a fee for bringing together the domestic seller and the overseas buyer.

expert witness A person with a special skill or experience in a business area, or professional knowledge of a specific subject.

export distributor A firm which usually has exclusive right to sell a manufacturer's products in all or some markets outside the United States.

Export-Import Bank Its main functions today are to give United States exporters the necessary financial backup to compete with other countries. This is done through a variety of different export financing and guarantee programs to meet specific needs. *See* Overseas Private Investment Corporation.

export letters of credit A source of credit support provided an exporter where the credit risk of the buyer is eliminated by the letter of credit.

export marketing A comprehensive approach to exploiting marketing opportunities in a foreign market involving target setting, product differentiation, and other factors.

export merchant Persons or firms that seek out needs in foreign markets and make purchases in the United States to fill these needs.

export selling The sale of goods manufactured in one country to customers in other countries. Typically, export selling involves independent distribution channels in the market country that are not managed by the manufacturer's marketing organization.

exposure to foreign exchange risk The amount of a person's or a business's holdings that is not denominated in the domestic currency, and whose value will fluctuate if foreign exchange rates vary.

express warranty The positive representation in oral or written form concerning the nature, quality, character, use, and purpose of goods which induce the buyer to buy.

extended coverage insurance Protection for the insured against property damage caused by windstorm, hail, smoke, explosion, riot, civil commotion, or vehicles and aircraft. This is provided in conjunction with the fire insurance policy and the various "package" policies.

extension The continuation past the original maturity date of a commitment.

external financing Providing for the financial needs of a company through outside sources, such as with bank loans or the sale of stock, as opposed to raising funds internally from profits.

extra dating When the vendor will allow extra or additional time for the purchaser to take the cash discount.

extraordinary item An expense or a revenue item, characterized by its unusual nature and infrequency of occurrence, which is shown net of tax effects separately from ordinary income on the income statement. Such items include plant abandonment, foreign-currency devaluation, and goodwill write-off.

F

face amount The nominal amount due at maturity from a bond or note.

face value of insurance In life insurance, refers to the amount of the death benefit of a policy, as opposed to the cash surrender or trade-in value.

facilitators Business organizations, such as transportation companies, warehouses, banks, and insurance companies, which assist in the logistical and final tasks of distribution but do not take title to goods or negotiate purchases or sales. *See* middleman.

facilities charge An amount to be paid by the electric system customer as a lump sum or periodically as reimbursement for facilities furnished. The charge may include operation and maintenance costs as well as fixed costs.

fact-finding An investigation by an authorized person or entity of a dispute by a public or private body. It examines the issues and facts in a case, and, as a result, may or may not recommend settlement procedures.

fact-finding board A special panel appointed to review the positions of labor and management in a particular dispute, with a view to analyzing the major issues in dispute and resolving, if possible, the differences as to the facts of the case. *See* conciliation.

factoring The business, usually conducted by a finance company, of buying accounts receivable at a discount. Outstanding accounts are bought by the factor, who then proceeds to collect the full amount from the debtor. *See* accounts receivable financing.

factory cost The manufacturing cost of an item, not including the cost of distribution.

facultative reinsurance A procedure by which insurance companies reinsure risks on an individual basis, with a reinsurer having the option to accept or decline each risk offered to him.

Fair Access to Insurance Requirements plan A facility, operating under a government insurance industry cooperative program, to make fire and other forms of property insurance readily available to persons who have difficulty obtaining such coverage.

fair competition Open competition between companies producing and marketing the same or similar products.

Fair Labor Standards Act A federal law which regulates the wages paid to employees by companies engaged in interstate commerce.

fair market price A value determined by bona fide arm's-length bargaining between well-informed buyers and sellers, usually over a period of time.

fair market purchase value The market value determined through arm's-length transaction between buyers and sellers.

fair market rental value The rental rate an asset would command in the open market in an arm's-length transaction.

fair value consideration A just compensation, under specific circumstances, paid for the sale or transfer of an item or property.

family corporation A corporation whose stock is held in the most part by members of one family.

Farm Credit Administration A unit in the U.S. Department of Agriculture whose responsibility it is to aid farmers during times of stress through the extension of credit and other financial assistance.

Farm Credit System The cooperative Farm Credit System provides credit and closely related services to farmers, ranchers, producers or harvesters of aquatic products, rural homeowners, and selected farm-related businesses. It also provides credit services to cooperatives whose members are farmers, ranchers, and producers or harvesters of aquatic products, and to associations of such cooperatives. The system serves all fifty states and Puerto Rico.

Farmers Home Administration In the U.S. Department of Agriculture, the Administration is an agency extending loans in rural areas for farms, homes, and community facilities.

farmowners-ranchowners policy A package policy for a farm or a ranch providing property and liability coverages against both personal and business losses.

fashion A currently accepted trend in a given field. Fashions tend to endure a period of time and pass through four stages: distinctiveness, emulation, mass fashion, and decline.

feasibility study An analysis designed to establish the practicality of a given project and if it appears advisable to do so, determine the direction of subsequent project efforts.

Federal Communications Commission The Commission has the power to regulate all interstate and foreign electric communications systems originating in the United States.

federal crime insurance Insurance against burglary, larceny, and robbery losses offered by the federal government, in cases where the Federal Insurance Administration has determined that such insurance is not otherwise readily available.

Federal Deposit Insurance Corporation An agency of the United States government that insures individual bank deposits and the solvency of banks.

Federal Financing Bank A federal institution which lends funds to a wide array of federal credit agencies by borrowing monies from the U.S. Treasury Department.

federal funds Funds held by the Federal Reserve member banks in excess of those needed to comply with legal reserve requirements. These funds are traded among member banks on a short-term basis, allowing those banks with more-than-necessary reserves to loan them on a day-to-day basis to banks with less-than-required reserves.

Federal Home Loan Banks The institutions that regulate and lend to savings and loan associations.

Federal Home Loan Mortgage Corporation Was established to help maintain the availability of mortgage credit for residential homes and maintain an active, nationwide secondary market in conventional residential mortgages. It purchases a large volume of conventional residential mortgages and sells them by means of mortgage-related investment instruments.

Federal Housing Administration Was established to encourage improvement in housing standards and conditions, to provide a system of mutual mortgage insurance as an aid to builders and buyers of homes and to mortgage-lending institutions, and for other purposes. It is also authorized to insure a variety of mortgage loans, mostly related to residential housing.

Federal Intermediate Credit Banks The banks make short- and intermediate-term loans to and discount paper for production credit associations, national and state banks, agricultural credit corporations, livestock loan companies, and similar financing institutions.

Federal Land Banks The stock of the twelve Federal Land Banks in the farmer-owned system is owned by approximately 520 Federal Land Bank associations through which borrowers apply for loans. Federal Land Bank loans are secured by first mortgages on rural real estate, and may be made to farmers and ranchers for a variety of agricultural purposes or other credit needs under the regulations of the Farm Credit Administration.

Federal Mediation and Conciliation Service An independent agency responsible for mediating and conciliating labor disputes in any industry affecting commerce other than those occurring in the railroad and air transportation industries.

Federal Trade Commission The Commission promotes free and fair competition in the American marketplace by enforcing the antitrust laws and similar statutes.

federal wire A communication system used to link member banks to the Federal Reserve System to settle payments for federal funds and for the settlement of payments of government securities.

feedback The flow of information back into the control monitor system so that actual performance can be compared with planned performance.

feedstock The primary raw material in a chemical or refining process normally received by pipeline or in large-scale bulk shipments. Feedstock availability is frequently the controlling factor in setting a production schedule and a rate for a process.

fidelity bond A form of coverage which reimburses an employer for losses caused by dishonest or fraudulent acts of employees.

fiduciary A person responsible for the custody or administration of property belonging to another. *See* trustee.

field warehouse receipt A receipt issued by a field warehouseman for inventory or for other property stored on the owner's premises.

file A collection of related records treated as a unit.

file management A computer system designed to provide a device-independent interface between a program and data stored on a disk.

filtering Screening out information from a system or from a communication network and sending in only certain specific data.

final assembly The manufacturing department where the product is assembled.

Financial Accounting Standards Board An independent board responsible for setting accounting principles since 1973.

financial leverage A financial structure having a large amount of debt and a relatively small amount of common stock equity; hence a small change in a company's or a project's earnings has a significant effect on earnings per share.

financial risk A corporation risk that is involved with both the possibility of insolvency and variations in earnings due to excessive fixed costs and interest payments to service short- and long-term debt obligations.

financial statement A balance sheet, an income statement, a funds statement, or any supporting statement or other presentation of final data derived from accounting records.

financing lease A form of lease in which a lessee can acquire the use of an asset for most of its useful life. Rental payments are net to the lessor, and the user of the asset is responsible for maintenance, taxes, and insurance. Rental payments over the life of the lease are sufficient to enable the lessor to recover the cost of the equipment plus a return on his investment. A finance lease may be either a true lease or a conditional sale. *See* true lease.

financing package A financial plan and commitments on a particular package. It could include options, limited partnerships, capital interests, and other elements required to carry the financing to completion.

financing statement Under the Uniform Commercial Code, this is an established form a lender files with the registrar of deeds or secretary of state. It gives the name and address of the debtor and the secured party (the lender), along with a description of the personal property securing the loan. It may show the amount of indebtedness.

finder A person who acts to bring together a purchaser and a vendor-seller and who is usually not in the employ of either. A finder usually is paid a fee by the party engaging his service, although the fee may be a percentage of the total transaction fee.

finished goods Manufactured products and completed products ready for sale.

fire insurance Coverage for losses caused by fire, lightning, and the removal of property from endangered premises, plus the damage caused by smoke and water.

firm commitment A lender's agreement to make a loan to a specific borrower on a specific property. Such commitment is usually good for a period of time before the closing of the transaction.

firm energy Electric energy which is intended to have assured availability to the customer in order to meet all or any agreed-upon portion of his load requirements.

first-in, first-out An inventory accounting method by which inventory values are determined from the most recent purchases and the cost of goods sold is determined from the oldest purchases. Commonly known as FIFO. *See* last-in, first-out (LIFO).

first mortgage A real estate loan that creates the first lien against real property. *See* senior debt.

first mortgage bonds Bonds secured by a first mortgage upon all or part of the property of the issuing organization. A first mortgage security on a given property is superior to any other security on the same property.

fiscal period A period of time used by a business as the length of its accounting cycle.

fiscal policy Federal government policies with respect to taxes, spending, and debt management, intended to promote the nation's economic goals, particularly with respect to employment, gross national product, price-level stability, and equilibrium in balance of payments.

fiscal year Any accounting period of twelve consecutive months chosen as the reporting period by a profit- or nonprofit-making entity. The federal fiscal year begins on October 1 and ends September 30.

fixed assets Plant or capital assets.

fixed cost (expense) An expense which does not vary in the short run with the volume of production.

fixed currency A currency whose official value is maintained by a central bank.

fixed liability Long-term liability.

flat rate In advertising, a uniform charge per unit of space in a medium without consideration of the amount of space used or of the frequency of insertion.

fleet policy A policy covering a number of motor vehicles owned by a single insured.

float Checks or money transfers that have been credited to the depositor's account at his bank but not yet debited to the drawer's account at his bank.

floater A form of insurance that applies to movable property, wherever its location, within the territorial limits imposed by the contract. The coverage "floats" with the property.

floating currency A currency whose exchange rate vis-à-vis those of other currencies is allowed to fluctuate relatively freely.

floating lending rate A lending rate which is established at a fixed number of percentage points above a given rate, such as the United States prime lending rate or the London Interbank Offer Rate (LIBOR), and which is renegotiated periodically.

floating-rate note A financial instrument tied to current money market rates and established under specified conditions for a period of time.

flood insurance Coverage against loss resulting from flood peril.

floor-load capacity The maximum weight that the floor of a building can safely support, expressed in pounds per square foot.

floor loan A portion of a mortgage loan commitment that is less than the full amount of the commitment. Specific events such as full occupancy must occur before the loan is funded in full. *See* gap financing.

flow chart A system-analysis tool to show graphically a procedure in which symbols are used to represent operations, data, flow, and equipment.

flower bonds Government bonds are acceptable at par for the payment of federal estate taxes when owned by the decedent at the time of death. *See* inheritance tax.

flow process chart Such charts are of two types: (1) the "material chart" represents the process in terms of events that occur to the material; and (2) the "man chart" presents the process in terms of activities of a given employee.

flow-through method An accounting procedure under which changes in state or federal income taxes resulting from the use of liberalized depreciation and the investment tax credit for income tax purposes are carried down to net income in the year in which they are realized.

fluctuation inventory An inventory that is carried as a cushion to protect against budgeting, planning, or forecasting errors. *See* maximum stock.

Food and Drug Administration A government agency with authority over the safety and purity of foods, drugs, cosmetics, and the labeling of products.

forbearance A delay in taking legal action for the nonpayment of debt service on a loan.

forced combination of advertising The joint sale of advertising for a morning and evening newspaper or other publication.

forced sale A sale made under the direction of the courts and in the mode prescribed by law.

forecast A reasonable prediction of the future based on data gathered in the past and the present. Such an analysis incorporates expected changes in the future as being different from events in the past.

foreclosure A legal procedure taken by a mortgagee or lender, under the terms of a mortgage or deed of trust, for the purpose of selling the property involved and applying the proceeds of the sale to the payment of a defaulted debt.

Foreign Agents Registration Act A federal law requiring people and organizations who represent foreign countries to register with the United States government so that their activities in behalf of such foreign countries can be followed.

foreign bill of exchange A certificate of exchange drawn in one country and payable in another country.

foreign bond Bond sold outside the country of the borrower, usually in the currency of the country in which the bond is issued. The bond is underwritten by local and international financial institutions, and is issued under the regulations prevalent in the country of issue.

foreign exchange Currency other than the one used domestically in a given country.

foreign exchange rate The intermarket relationship between the currencies of two countries.

foreign exchange risk A financial risk which may be present for holding or hedging certain currencies. The adverse movement of relevant exchange rates may increase the risks involved.

foreign freight forwarders Specialists in traffic operations, overseas import regulations, customs clearances, and shipping rates and schedules. They also assist manufacturers or combination export managers in determining and paying freight costs, fees, and insurance charges.

foreign marketing A marketing management approach which takes into account the laws, customs, and markets of a foreign country and develops a comprehensive plan for selling a product or a service to that country.

foreman Generally, the first line of management in the operation of the plant or facility, and the immediate supervisor of a group of workers with the responsibility for recommending suspension, discharge, or promotion.

forfeiture The loss of money or collateral due to a failure to perform in a manner established prior to a specific event.

formal organization The structure of a business or government agency in which individuals are given authority and responsibility to perform the specific tasks assigned to them. *See* informal organization.

FORTRAN (Formula Translation) A computer language used in mathematical, scientific, and engineering problem areas.

forward delivery The delivery of financial instruments and securities to satisfy cash or futures market transactions of an earlier date.

forward integration A management plan involved in a company's seeking ownership or increased control of some of its dealers or distributors.

forward market A market in which participants agree to trade some commodity, security, or foreign exchange at a fixed price for delivery at some future date.

forward rate Foreign exchange rate established in the present for currency to be delivered at a future date.

franchise The authorization to do business using the name and operating methods established by another enterprise. Also, governments may grant franchises for providing services in their political jurisdiction.

franchisee The firm that receives the franchise from a business or government body.

franchiser The parent company that franchises firms to sell their products. Also, a government agency which selects firms to provide services in specific areas of the political jurisdiction.

franchise tax A tax on the right and privilege of a corporation to carry out its business.

franchising An arrangement whereby a firm or a government body licenses a company with exclusive rights to sell its products or to provide services in a specific territory.

free alongside ship In shipping, the seller is obligated to deliver the goods alongside the overseas vessel at the named port, within reach of the ship's loading tackle.

freehold The ownership of land.

free on board In this delivery contract, the responsibility and liability of the seller does not end until the goods actually have been placed aboard a ship.

free port A restricted area at a seaport for the handling of duty-exempted import goods; a "foreign trade zone."

free-rein leadership A management approach which considers that the less supervision the better for the objectives of the company.

free riders Employees who do not belong to a contract-holding union (but who are eligible for membership), who do not pay dues or other fees and assessments to the union, but who receive the benefits of the union's activities in collective bargaining and grievance and arbitration handling.

freight forwarder A company engaged in consolidating, documenting, and otherwise handling domestic or foreign shipments.

frequency distribution A table that indicates the frequency with which data fall into each of any number of subdivisions of the variable.

fringe benefits Nonwage benefits or payments received by workers. They include such items as vacation pay, paid sick leave, paid holidays, pensions, and insurance benefits. *See* sick benefits.

fringe time (television) The approximately one-hour period adjacent to prime time.

frontage The line of one's property that faces the street or highway.

front-end money The soft costs required to start a development. These funds are made available to the developer or equity owner as a capital contribution to the project. *See* developer.

fuel adjustment clause A clause in an electric rate schedule that provides for an adjustment of the customer's bill if the cost of fuel at the supplier's generating stations varies from a specified unit cost.

fuel replacement energy Electric energy generated at a hydroelectric plant as a substitute for energy which would otherwise have been generated by a thermoelectric plant.

full dilution Earnings per share calculated on a basis that assumes the issuance of stock shares to satisfy all outstanding warrants, convertibles, or other claims which potentially increase the number of shares of common stock.

full disclosure Revealing all the facts about a subject; particularly pertinent when a corporate or other entity sells securities to the public.

full faith and credit A pledge of the general taxing power for the payment of debt obligations. Bonds carrying such pledges are usually referred to as general obligation bonds or full faith and credit bonds. *See* general obligation bond.

function In business, a job, task, or process. In computer programming, mathematical economics, or statistics, an algebraic expression describing the relation between two or more variables, the function taking on a definite value, when special values are assigned to the argument(s), or independent variable(s), or the function.

functional accounts Groupings of plant and expense accounts according to the specified function or part they play in the operations of the business.

functional authority A delegation of specific authority to a person in a line responsibility. Such authority could limit or designate only those specific areas for which authority is granted by a superior.

functional organization An organization plan which uses the designation of specialized authority. This type of organization has characteristics of both line and staff functions.

fund An asset or group of assets separated from others in the accounts and limited to specific uses.

fundamental research In security analysis, the examination of industries and companies based on such factors as sales, assets, earnings, products, or on services, markets, and management. As applied to the economy, fundamental research includes the consideration of gross national product, interest rates, money supply, unemployment, inventories, savings, and other areas.

furlough A leave of absence from work or other duties, usually initiated by an employee to meet some special problem. *See* attrition.

future advance Disbursement of funds after the execution of a mortgage.

futures Contracts which require the delivery of a commodity or security of a specified quality and quantity, at a specified price, on a specified future date. Futures are traded on various exchanges and are used for both speculation and hedging.

futures market An organized market in which contracts for the future delivery of a commodity or a security are bought and sold.

G

gainful occupation In compensation insurance, a term used to determine whether an injured person could continue his ordinary occupation or employment.

gantt chart A technique for planning, control, and general management, showing by bars on a chart the time requirements for the various tasks or events of a production or other program.

gap financing An interim loan to finance the difference between the floor loan and the maximum permanent loan committed by the lender. *See* floor loan.

garnishment A legal proceeding that applies specified monies, wages, or property to a debt or debtor to pay back the obligations of a debtor.

General Accounting Office A federal agency reporting to the U.S. Congress, headed by the Comptroller General and responsible for accounting and auditing funds of the United States government. *See* Comptroller General.

general creditor A creditor with priority for payment during bankruptcy.

general fund A fund used to account for all transactions of a governmental unit which are not accounted for in another fund.

general liability insurance A form of coverage that pertains to claims arising out of the liability for injuries or damage caused by ownership of property, manufacturing operations, contracting operations, sale or distribution of products, and providing professional services.

generally accepted accounting principles The broadly interpreted principles and guidelines of the accounting profession. The presentation of a company's financial data, which guides the accountant in the proper treatment of a company's financial transactions.

general mortgage bond A bond secured by all of the issuing company's property which is not pledged for other bond issues.

general obligation bond A bond issued by state and local governments and secured by the unlimited taxing power of the political jurisdiction. *See* full faith and credit.

general partner Member of a partnership who is liable for all debts of the partnership, contrasted with a limited partner, who is liable to the extent of his contributed capital. *See* limited partner.

General Services Administration A federal government agency which supplies all government offices with supplies, office space, and other materials.

gift tax The tax imposed on the transfer of property from one living person to another.

giveback A previously won union gain which is subsequently relinquished to management after contract negotiations.

give up In bond market trading, the loss in yield that occurs when a block of bonds is swapped for another block of lower-coupon bonds.

Glass-Steagall Act An act of Congress which separates the functions of investment banking firms and commercial banks. In essence, commercial banks are forbidden to underwrite or deal in corporate securities and municipal revenue bonds.

go-between An intermediary who serves as the agent between two parties engaged in negotiating a transaction.

going and coming rule Injuries suffered while going to work or coming home from work. May or may not be covered by the insurance of the employer. *See* workmen's compensation laws.

going concern A business enterprise which is assumed to remain in operation until all current plans are carried out as expected.

going concern accounting concept A principle of accounting which assumes, for normal presentation of financial data, that a business will keep operating and not be liquidated or sold.

going public A business procedure when a privately held company issues stocks or other debt obligations for purchase by the general public. *See* prospectus.

good delivery A condition which must exist prior to the transfer of property or security, and usually necessitates documentation as to title, legal opinions, proper price, and other requirements.

goods Items of merchandise, raw material, or finished goods. Sometimes include all tangible items, as in goods and services.

goodwill The excess of cost paid for an acquired firm over the current value of net assets of the acquired company. The good name and reputation of the company.

government bond Securities issued by the federal government in order to finance obligations and programs approved by the executive and legislative branches of the government. The bonds are usually issued in coupon form and are of various maturity.

government-guaranteed loans Loans for which the federal government guarantees in whole or in part the repayment of principal and/or interest.

government-sponsored enterprises Enterprises with completely private ownership, such as Federal Land Banks and Federal Home Loan Banks, established and chartered by the federal government to perform specialized functions. These enterprises are not included in the budget totals and are considered off-balance-sheet items.

grace period A period beyond the due date of a premium during which insurance is continued in force and during which payment must be made to keep the policy in good standing.

graduated lease A lease providing for a variable rental rate, sometimes set forth in the lease, sometimes determined by a reappraisal using a predetermined formula; also applicable for graduated payment mortgages.

graduated payment mortgage (GPM) Has scheduled monthly payments that start out at a low level, compared with those of a standard fixed payment mortgage, but rise later. The graduation rate, the term of graduation, and the interest rate are fixed throughout the life of the loan.

grandfather lease A lease entered into within ninety days of the signing of the Economic Recovery Tax Act of 1981, concerning property which was placed in service in 1981 prior to the Act.

grantee The person or corporation to whom an interest in real property is conveyed.

grantor The person or corporation conveying an interest in real property.

grid system A utility's power generation, transmission, and distribution system, including transmission lines and transformer stations.

grievance A complaint made by an employee, or his union representative, against an employer because he may have been wronged in some area or aspect of his employment.

grievance procedure The formal steps established in a contract for the effective handling of complaints made by employees or employers against each other.

gross income The total income or receipts of a person or business, prior to deducting expenses.

gross margin Sales minus cost of products sold. It may be expressed as a percentage of net sales.

gross national product The market value of the goods and services produced by the labor and property supplied by residents of the United States before deduction of depreciation charges and other allowances for business and institutional consumption of capital goods. Other business products used up by business are deducted. The gross national product comprises the purchase of goods and services by consumers and government, gross private domestic investment (including the change in business inventories), and net exports (exports less imports).

gross private domestic investment Fixed capital goods purchased by private business and nonprofit institutions, and the change in business inventories.

gross profit The excess of the price paid for goods and products before deductions are made for the cost of operation.

gross spread The difference between the price that the issuer receives for its securities and the price investors pay for them. This spread equals the sales concession plus the management and underwriting fees and expenses.

ground lease Contract for the rental of land, usually on a long-term basis.

group banking A term used to describe a form of banking enterprise whereby a group of existing banks form a holding company. The holding company supervises all the banks in the group and coordinates their operations through uniform procedures.

group discount A special discount in rates for the simultaneous use of a company's services by groups of persons. Applicable in advertising, travel, entertainment, and other areas.

group insurance Any insurance plan under which a number of persons and their dependents are insured under a single policy, issued to their employer or to an association with which they are affiliated, with individual certificates given to each insured person.

guaranteed annual wage A labor contract in which an employer agrees to pay an employee a certain basic sum of money each year regardless of the way the employee is paid or the level of production activity by and need for such an employee.

guaranteed employment A program, instituted by an employer or by joint negotiation with a union, assuring workers a specified number of hours of work per week or number of weeks per year.

guaranty A written promise by a person or corporation to pay a debt or perform an obligation contracted by another in the event that the original obligor fails to pay or perform as contracted.

H

hail insurance Coverage for loss or damage to growing crops due to hail.

haircut transaction In a government repurchase transaction, the difference between the market value and the stated value of the repurchase agreement.

half run In transit advertising, a car card placed in every other unit of the transit system used.

handle In money market trading, the dollar price of the security as traded in the current market.

handling charge A fee charged by intermediaries for rendering services to a client.

hard copy A printed copy of machine output in a visually readable form, such as printed reports, listings, documents, and summaries.

hardware In the computer field, the mechanical and electronic processing equipment.

harvesting strategy A marketing strategy in which the firm sharply reduces its current expenses to increase its current profits. This may generate a reduction in sales and a diminution of the market share of the product.

hazard A condition which creates or increases the chances of a loss.

hazard pay Special remuneration or compensation paid for work under uncomfortable or unpleasant conditions, or for work which endangers the life or health of the worker.

health insurance Insurance against financial losses resulting from sickness or bodily injury. Could be paid in part by the employer and in part by the employee.

hedge A financial technique used to minimize risks by taking contrary positions in a security transaction in the present and, at times, for future consideration. *See* arbitrage.

held in trust A legal position when a property is held by a third party for the benefit of another entity. The specific guidelines and direction given to the trustee are used to manage and control the property kept in trust.

hell-or-high-water clause A contractual provision which stipulates that the payment specified in the contract must be paid under any conditions to the contrary. Generally, the obligor becomes the credit backing for the contract, since he is fully responsible for the specified payments.

heuristic A form of problem solving where the results or rules have been determined by rule of thumb or intuition instead of by optimization.

hidden offers In advertising, a special offer incorporated inconspicuously in the copy of a print advertisement which may result in much attention to the product offered in the ad.

hierarchy of needs The motivation of persons, which ranges from meeting lower-level needs to achieving higher-level needs, from personal safety to self-actualization.

highest and best use The use that will produce the highest present property value and develop a site to its full economic potential.

histogram A graphic display used in statistical presentations. A series of rectangles, one of which is erected above each class interval. The width of each rectangle represents the width of the class interval, and its height the number of cases or frequencies in the class.

historical cost accounting An accounting approach in which financial statements reflect only historical transaction prices without regard to replacement cost. This is the most widely used accounting technique.

holdback A portion of a loan commitment (at times an amount equal to the contractor's profit) not funded until some additional requirement such as rental or completion is attained.

hold harmless agreement A contract under which one party's legal liability for damages is assumed by the other party to the contract or by an outside insurer.

holding company A corporation organized for the purpose of owning stock in and managing one or more other corporations.

holdover audience The television or radio audience inherited from the show immediately preceding the one being watched or listened to.

homeowners association An organization of homeowners residing within a particular development whose major purpose is to maintain and provide community facilities and services for the common enjoyment of the residents. Usually the association levies a fee or charge for these services.

homeowners policy A package type of insurance for the homeowner, which includes coverages ranging from fire and extended coverage to theft and personal liability.

horizontal diversification This action takes place when new products are created that could appeal to a company's current customers although they are technically unrelated to its current product line.

horizontal integration A company action in which it seeks ownership or increased control of some of its competitors. *See* vertical integration.

horizontal publications An industrial or a trade publication which reaches persons at a certain level in all industries.

house mark A primary mark or designation of a business concern, usually used with the trademark of its products.

house organ A magazine, newspaper, or other publication issued periodically by a company to its employees to keep them informed about the company, its products and operation, and the activities of other employees.

hull policy A contract that provides indemnification for damage to or loss of an insured vessel or airplane.

human-oriented language A programming language that is more like a human language than a machine language.

hydro A term used to identify a type of generating station or a power or energy output in which the prime mover is driven by water power.

hydroenergy potential The aggregate energy capable of being developed over a specified period by practicable use of the available streamflow and river gradient.

hypothecate To pledge property as security for a loan without giving up actual title. The property is used as collateral. Very common in margin accounts where the securities are used to secure a broker's loan. *See* pledged asset.

I

idle time A time period in the manufacturing process when operators or machines are not turning out the product because of setup, poor maintenance, lack of material, tooling, or change of shifts.

image The set of beliefs which a person or group holds about a phenomenon.

implementation A process of installing a system or project into operation. Generally, a function of a project manager to implement a task according to schedule and within budgetary requirements.

implied consideration Payment or reward for certain actions taken without prior contractual agreement of a promise to pay.

impoundment Any action or inaction by an officer or employee of the United States that precludes the obligation or expenditure of budget authority provided by the U.S. Congress. Generally most visible when funds are impounded by the President.

improved land Land having utilities, roads, or other infrastructural items.

impulse buying A purchase made without preplanning; instinctive buying.

imputed cost Cost and expense items which are indirectly estimated and which are attributed rather than directly measured.

in bond The storage or transport of goods in the custody of a warehouse or carrier from whom the goods can be taken by a legally authorized person only upon payment of taxes or duties to a governmental agency.

incentive construction contract A contract that specifies extra rewards for better-than-contracted performance, such as lower costs, more rapid completion of work, or other factors.

incentive labor contracts Clauses in collective bargaining agreements which establish systems of incentive wage payments and specify the process through which these incentives are to be extended to new groups that may come within the bargaining unit.

income Excess of revenues over expenses for a period of time. Income may be from rentals, commissions, royalties, interest, and other sources.

income and expense statement The actual or estimated schedule of income and expense items reflecting net gain or loss during a specified period.

income approach to value The appraisal technique used to estimate real-property value by capitalizing net income.

income bond A bond on which interest is paid only if the issuer is profitable. An income bond is thus very similar to preferred stock, both of which may have a cumulative clause.

income property A property in which the income is derived from commercial rentals, such as retail or office space.

income statement A summary of the revenues and expenses of an enterprise prepared for a specified period of time.

income tax An annual tax levied by the federal government and by many state and local governments on the income of a corporate entity, person, or partnership.

incontestable clause A covenant in a life insurance policy stating that the insurance company may not contest a policy, or one of its provisions, after the coverage has been in force for a period of time.

incorporate To establish a corporation or carry out a business under a corporate name; a legal and financial structure.

incremental cost In production or manufacturing, the cost added in the process of finishing a part or an assembly, assembling a group of parts, or adding parts or assemblies to a more advanced level of preparation. *See* marginal cost.

incremental energy costs The additional cost of producing and/or transmitting electric energy above some base cost previously determined.

indemnity agreement A contract provision in which one party agrees to insure another party against anticipated and specified losses.

indenture A written contract under which bonds or debentures are issued, setting forth maturity date, interest rate, security, and other terms. There is usually a third-party trustee for the indenture who has the right to carry out the provisions of the contract.

indenture trustee The indenture trustee holds the security interest in the property for the benefit of the lenders and bondholders. In the event of default, the indenture trustee exercises the rights of lenders.

independent contractor A person or a corporation which is providing specified services to another without outside control except as it relates to the nature of the contractual employment.

indexing Adjusting wages, pensions, mortgages, or other debt issues by some measure of inflation to preserve the purchasing power of future benefits and investment earnings in constant monetary units.

index of help-wanted advertising volume A statistical measure based on the number of help-wanted ads published in the classified sections of leading newspapers—drawn from cities located throughout the country, representing the major labor market areas.

indirect costs Costs, such as overhead costs, which are not easily associated with the production of specific goods and services. *See* direct costs.

indirect labor A cost which is not specifically charged to any operation or department, but is an expense associated with the general operation of the plant or organization. *See* direct labor.

individual brand A manufacturer's policy of distributing each of his products under a specific and unique brand name.

individual markup The markup designated on each individual item, expressed in both dollars and percent.

indivisible contract A legal agreement which may not be separated and in which all parts must be exercised in order to comply with the contractual requirements. *See* divisible contract.

industrial advertising Oriented to manufacturers who buy machinery, equipment, raw materials, and components needed to make industrial and commercial products.

industrial dynamics An interactive approach to management planning and control in which flows of information, materials, labor, capital equipment, and money are seen as an interrelated system influencing the growth, fluctuation, and decline of a business.

industrial goods Raw materials, machines, and tools which are utilized for the production of other goods.

industrial production index Measures changes in the physical volume or quantity of the output of manufacturers, mining operations, and electric and gas utilities. It reflects output changes at all stages within manufacturing and mining industries. The index is prepared by the Federal Reserve System. *See* consumer price index.

industrial revenue bonds Issued by governmental units, the proceeds of which are used to construct plant facilities for private industrial and commercial concerns. Debt-service payments made in accordance to a lease by the industrial concern to the governmental unit are used to service the bonds.

industrial unions Unions whose membership is determined by the nature of the industry, such as mine workers. *See* craft unions.

inflation A continuous and unregulated upward movement of general price levels, which may develop from such causes as a limited supply of goods and services or an increasing supply of money or credit. Inflation is also characterized by a decline in the present buying power of the dollar in relation to previous periods. *See* stagflation.

informal organization A system based on the interpersonal relationships of workers that exists within the framework of the formal organizational structure. *See* formal organization.

information retrieval The furnishing of information rapidly to the place where it is needed.

infringement of copyright A reproduction of a substantial amount of a copyrighted book or article.

infringement of patent An unauthorized use of a presented invention.

infringement of trademark A violation or imitation of a trademark developed for specific goods or services.

inheritance tax A tax imposed on the transfer or passing of money or property by legacy or succession. *See* flower bonds.

initial markup The markup originally placed on the merchandise when it was offered for sale.

injunction A court order obtained by a person or entity to prohibit another from performing some act.

inland marine insurance A type of insurance, generally covering articles that may be transported from one place to another as well as covering bridges, tunnels, and other forms of transportation and communication.

input Putting information and data into a system or computer for processing and decision making.

insecurity clause A contractual provision allowing a creditor to force the entire payment due from the debtor.

inserts (freestanding) The loose inserts placed between the pages or sections of a newspaper.

inserts (magazine) A reply card or other printed piece such as a coupon inserted in a magazine opposite the advertiser's full-page advertisement.

insolvency The inability to pay debts when due. *See* default.

inspection Checking for defective products in the quality-control process.

inspection laws Laws requiring the examination of various kinds of merchandise intended for sale, especially foods, with a view to determining fitness for use.

installment The regular, periodic partial payment that a borrower agrees to make to the lender.

installment method Recognizing revenue and expense in proportion to the fraction of the installment payment collected during a period of time.

installment note A note requiring the periodic payment of a specified sum to satisfy a debt.

installment sales contracts Agreements in which a customer agrees to pay for a purchase by paying a certain amount of money on a regular basis for a preset period of time.

institutional advertising Advertising intended to build goodwill and public support for the advertiser rather than stimulate the immediate purchase of a product or service.

institutional investor An organization whose primary purpose is to invest in equity or debt instruments. It invests its own assets or those held in trust by it for others. Includes pension funds, investment companies, insurance companies, universities, and banks.

institutional lender A financial institution that invests in debt instruments and carries them in its own portfolio. Insurance companies, banks, bond funds, trust funds, and pension funds are examples of these institutions.

instrument A formal legal document, such as a lease, a mortgage, a negotiable security, a contract, a will, or a deed.

insufficient funds A bank term meaning that the drawer's deposit balance is smaller than the amount of a check presented for payment. The payment of such a check would result in an overdraft on the depositor's account.

insurable interest An interest or event, if not insured against, which would cause financial loss or other damages to the insured.

insurance A legal and financial device for reducing risks via the payment of premiums. The beneficiary of the insurance is guaranteed a compensation in certain events, i.e., when losses occur.

insurance guaranty fund A fund usually established by state law, derived from assessments of solvent insurance companies and used to absorb losses of claimants against insolvent insurers.

insurance to value Insurance written in an amount approximating the value of the property insured.

insured mortgage loan A loan insured by the Federal Housing Administration or a private mortgage insurance company.

intangible asset Any nonphysical asset, such as a patent, a trademark, or goodwill.

interactive system Refers to those computer applications in which a user communicates with a computer program via a terminal, entering data and receiving responses from the computer.

Inter-American Development Bank The Bank is owned by the governments of twenty-six regional and fifteen nonregional countries. Its purpose is to further the economic and social development of its regional developing member countries, individually and collectively.

interchange energy Electric energy received by one electric utility system usually in exchange for energy delivered to another system at another time or place. Interchange energy should be distinguished from a direct purchase or sale of such power supplies, although accumulated energy balances are sometimes paid for in cash.

interest The charge or cost for using money, frequently expressed as an annual interest rate for a fixed term, or the rate may vary with money market rates, such as the prime lending rate.

interest equalization tax A tax imposed on United States residents who purchased foreign securities between 1963 and 1973.

intergovernmental revenue Revenue received from other governments in the form of grants, shared revenues, or payments in lieu of taxes.

interim financing Short-term financing during the time a project is commenced to the closing of a permanent loan or mortgage, usually in the form of a construction loan and/or a development loan. *See* permanent loan.

interlocking directorates If two firms are in direct competition, one person may not serve on the boards of directors of the two companies.

intermediate debt Debt having a maturity range from five to ten years.

intermittent production A process wherein orders are produced to meet customers' specifications. Also called a job-lot form of production. *See* continuous production.

internal audit A relatively independent audit conducted by employees for managerial purposes to determine how control procedures are working.

internal control The management tasks carried out by certain executives of a business to attempt to ensure that operations are carried out as planned.

internal financing Providing for the financial requirements of a company through any inside sources which may be available, such as from retained profits.

internal rate of return The discount rate that equates the net present value of a stream of cash outflows with the net present value of cash inflows to zero. *See* average rate of return.

Internal Revenue Service A unit of the U.S. Treasury Department which administers the tax code and collects the taxes received by the federal government.

International Bank for Reconstruction and Development (World Bank) The principal purpose of the Bank is to promote the economic development of its member countries, primarily by providing loans for specific projects and related technical assistance, in the interest of promoting the long-term growth of international trade and improved standards of living.

international marketing When a national firm conducts business in foreign markets.

International Monetary Fund A Fund established by a large number of countries for the purpose of creating a liquid supply of international lendable resources.

Interstate Commerce Act A federal law designed to regulate commerce between the states, and particularly the transportation of persons and property by carriers between interstate points. *See* commerce power.

interview The face-to-face contact between the company representative and the job applicant.

intestate The state of dying without having made a will. The estate is presented for settlement to administrators or other legally authorized parties.

in-the-money option A market condition when the market price of the underlying stock has risen above the strike price of the option. *See* out-of-the-money option.

intrinsic value A professional valuation which is valid by the facts or the underlying assumptions in a specific examination.

inventory Items which are in stock or work-in-process. Inventories may consist of finished goods ready for sale, or they may be parts or intermediate items.

inventory control A function that strives to maintain adequate materials while minimizing inventory carrying costs.

inventory turnover The cost of goods sold during a period of time divided by the average inventory for the period.

investment A current expenditure made to acquire assets or properties in anticipation of future income.

investment banker A firm that engages in the origination, underwriting, trading, and marketing of new issues, of mergers and acquisitions, arbitrage, secondary market trading, and provides other financial services. *See* merchant bank.

investment company A corporation or trust through which investors pool their funds to obtain diversification and management of their investments. There are two types of companies: (1) closed-end and (2) open-end funds. *See* mutual fund.

investment securities Stocks, bonds, and other securities sold on organized exchanges or through the over-the-counter market in accordance with standards established by the Securities and Exchange Commission and other regulatory bodies.

investment tax credit (ITC) A reduction in income tax liability granted by the federal government to firms that buy new equipment and livestock. *See* leverage lease.

investment tax credit indemnity An agreement by the lessee which commits to reimburse the lessor for any financial loss incurred through the loss of, or inability to claim, any or all of the anticipated equipment investment tax credit and other tax benefits.

investment tax credit strip lease A type of nominal lease in which the lessor claims only investment tax credit and not tax depreciation. If allowed by tax law, it is useful for a corporate entity with a large tax liability in one year.

investment trust A corporate entity in business to invest its assets in securities and distribute income and profits from these investments under specific rules and covenants agreed to by the directors of the trust.

investor-owned electric utilities These utilities, which may be held by an individual proprietor or a small group of people, are usually corporations owned by the general public. *See* municipally owned electric system.

invoice A document showing the details of a sale.

involuntary lien A lien imposed against property without the consent of an owner. Examples include taxes, special assessments, federal income tax liens, judgment liens, mechanic's liens, and materials liens.

ira (individual retirement account) A pension plan where accumulated funds are tax deferred until retirement and cannot be withdrawn without penalty before the retirement date as specified in the Federal tax law. A plan may be established by an individual regardless of his participation in a corporate pension program.

irrevocable letter of credit A financial security device which cannot be modified or rescinded without express permission by all parties. *See* revocable letter of credit.

island display A store display fixture centered in an open space.

island position On a publication page, a format in which an advertisement is surrounded entirely by editorial matter.

issue A financial function when a corporation exchanges its authorized stocks or bonds for cash or other assets.

issuing bank The bank that issues a letter of credit or other credit facility. *See* letter of credit.

J

jingle An advertisement set to music, usually carrying the slogan or theme line of a campaign. The objective is to make a brand name or slogan better remembered.

job analysis A complete review of a particular job or position in order to determine the facts about it, including methods or procedures of work, tools, responsibilities, supervision, standards of output, and other data concerning the technical nature of the work.

jobber A middleman or dealer who purchases goods or commodities from manufacturers, importers, or wholesalers and sells them to retailers.

job classification A stratification of work positions by class, level of difficulty, and other factors.

job description An analysis of the duties to be performed on a job, and of the qualifications needed by the person who will hold that position.

job dilution A procedure for subdividing the various parts or components of a highly skilled job into individual, separate skilled, semiskilled, and unskilled portions.

job enlargement An expansion of the job content with a view to making it less specialized and presumably more interesting and challenging.

job enrichment Programs for building into jobs a high sense of meaning, challenge, and potential for accomplishment.

job evaluation An organized method of determining the value of each job in relation to other jobs in the firm.

job grading The process of establishing various classes of jobs according to their relative importance.

job rotation A policy used in some companies to provide an opportunity for employees to become familiar with a variety of operations in the firm.

job shop An organization whose work centers are arranged around particular types of equipment or operations, such as drilling, forging, spinning, or assembly. Products flow through departments in batches corresponding to individual orders, which may be either in stock orders or specific customer orders.

job specification A detailed list of the personal qualifications needed for each job.

joint account An agreement, informal or written, between two or more firms to share risk and financing responsibilities in purchasing or underwriting securities.

joint liability The sharing of responsibility among more than one person or firm. In the event of a suit, the firms act as codefendants.

joint rate A rate agreed upon by two or more carriers and applying between two points. Such a rate may include one or more intermediate carriers in its route.

joint-stock company A voluntary association of persons operating under articles of agreement, with capital divided into transferable shares.

joint tenancy An estate in real property held by two or more persons as a unit and as one tenant. Upon the death of one joint tenant, his property passes to the survivor or survivors named in the joint tenancy.

joint venture An association between two or more parties to own and/or develop a project. It may take a variety of legal forms, including a partnership, tenancy in common, or a corporation. It is formed for a specific purpose and duration. Risks, tax benefits, equity contributions, and other factors can be divided and allocated based on a joint-venture agreement.

journal A record of the original entry of accounting transactions, with such entries kept in chronological order and ultimately posted to the various accounts contained in the ledger.

journal entry A record kept in or prepared for a book of original entry, interpreting a business transaction in bookkeeping terms and showing the accounts to be debited and credited, together with an explanatory description of the transaction.

journeyman A qualified, skilled tradesman who has completed a special apprenticeship program and mastered a specific skill or craft.

junior mortgage A subordinated lien that is subsequent to the claims of the holder of a prior (senior) mortgage. *See* second mortgage.

junk bonds High-risk bonds that have low credit ratings or are in or near default. These bonds usually sell at a deep discount.

jurisdictional dispute A controversy between unions as to which has the right over certain types of work activities or procedures, including the right to represent workers.

jurisdictional strike A work stoppage resulting from a dispute over jurisdictional claims by two competing unions.

[illegible]

[illegible]

[illegible]

[illegible]

journey [illegible]

[illegible]

hand position [illegible]

[illegible]

[illegible]

K

Keogh plan A private-sector pension program, established by federal law, allowing self-employed businessmen and professionals to set up pension and retirement plans for themselves. *See* pension plan.

key-man insurance Life insurance on an important, or "key," executive, generally purchased by his company, with the company named as the beneficiary.

key personnel Individuals in a business enterprise who are responsible for the overseeing of important functions, or whose particular jobs are such that others are unable to perform their work without them.

kickback A form of extortion which may be perpetrated by labor leaders, employers, or suppliers. *See* embezzlement.

kidnap and ransom insurance Insurance to cover the cost of ransom or extortion payments and related expenses.

kilowatt (kw) 1,000 watts.

kilowatt-hour (kwh) The basic unit of electric energy equal to one kilowatt of power supplied to or taken from an electric circuit steadily for one hour.

kurtosis In statistical analysis, the state or quality of the shape of a distribution related to its flatness or peakedness.

K

[illegible]

kilowatt hour (kwh). The basic unit of electric [illegible] one thousand watts of power supplied for [illegible] [illegible] for the home.

[illegible]

L

labor dispute A labor disagreement, which may include a dispute between parties concerning a collective bargaining agreement over the terms or the interpretation of the terms of their contract.

labor intensive Labor-intensive products use proportionately more labor than other elements in their production. Handmade goods with a low materials content are produced by a labor-intensive process. Service industries are usually labor intensive.

labor turnover The general measure of turnover in a particular plant or industry is a percentage which is derived from a fraction, the numerator being the number of separations from the plant and the denominator the average number of employees on the payroll.

labor union An association of workmen who have joined together for securing better working conditions, wages, and fringe benefits.

lagging indicators In economic analysis, those time series that tend to follow or trail behind aggregate economic activity. *See* coincident indicators; leading indicators.

land grant A donation of public lands to a government, a corporation, or an individual, usually from the United States government to a state or local government.

landlord's lien A direct claim by the landlord or a managing agent to the property of a tenant who has not paid his rent.

land tax A tax laid upon the legal or beneficial owner of real property and upon the assessed value of his land.

Lanham Act The federal statute governing trademarks and other symbols identifying products sold in interstate commerce.

last-in, first-out An inventory-flow assumption, where the cost of goods sold is the cost of the most recently acquired units, and the inventory cost is the sum of costs of the oldest units. Commonly referred to as LIFO. *See* first-in, first-out. (FIFO).

leadership The skill of influencing and motivating people so that they will strive willingly toward the achievement of group goals.

leading indicators In economic analysis, those time series that tend to move ahead of aggregate economic activity, reaching peaks and troughs before the economy as a whole does. *See* coincident indicators; lagging indicators.

leads and lags (currency) A currency trading technique of quickly moving funds into a given currency (lead) or delaying the movement of funds into a given currency (lag) with the objective of benefiting from expected changes in exchange rates.

lead time A span of time required to perform an activity. Also, the time required for the procurement of materials and/or products either from an outside supplier or from one's own manufacturing facility.

learning curve A management tool which represents graphically the relationship between efficiency and experience. The greater the experience of a worker in performing a given task, the greater savings in the per-unit cost of labor required to manufacture or produce a product.

lease An agreement containing the conditional requirements under which the possession and use of real and/or personal property are given by the owner to another for a stated period of time and for a stated consideration.

lease agreement A contractual arrangement in which an owner transfers the use of property or equipment, subject to specified terms and conditions, to another for a prescribed period of time and rental rate.

leaseback A sale of land or property with a lease given by the purchaser back to the original owner. Thus, the original owner stays on as a user of the property.

leasehold A lease of property or estate for a fixed period of time, usually for several years.

lease-leaseback A transaction used to achieve an investment tax credit strip lease. The first lease includes a pass-through of the investment tax credit benefits. The leaseback defines tax and legal ownership and the right to claim tax depreciation.

lease rate The equivalent simple annual interest rate implicit in minimum lease rentals.

lease term The duration of the lease, which includes, for accounting purposes, all periods covered by fixed-rate renewal options that are likely to be exercised at the start of the lease.

least-and-latest taxing rule Under this rule, one pays the least amount of tax as late as possible as is allowed by law. Penalties apply if payment is late, but the interest rates charged by the government may be less than the prevailing money market rates.

ledger A book of accounts.

legal investments Investments which savings banks, insurance companies, trustees, government entities, and other fiduciaries are permitted to make according to the laws of the states in which they carry out their business. The investments which meet the conditions imposed by law constitute the legal investment list. Also known as legal lists.

legal opinion Any opinion of a lawyer accepted by the parties who require it. The opinion could be from an attorney general, a city attorney, or an outside counsel. In the case of municipal bonds, investors require the opinion of a specialized bond attorney as to the legality of a bond issue.

lessee The user of equipment or property which is the subject of a lease agreement.

lessor The owner of equipment or property which is the subject of a lease agreement.

let An award or a contract to one of the bidders, as in "to let a contract."

letter of credit An instrument or a document sent from one party (usually a bank) to another concerning funds which will be made available upon completion of some business transactions. Usually, a buyer sends a letter of credit to the seller of goods when buyer and seller are not known to each other. Upon certification of the shipment of the goods in question and the submission of a draft, the bank may arrange for funds to be made available to the exporter. *See* issuing bank.

level payments Equal payments over the term of the lease. Usually rent and debt service are paid on a level-payment basis.

leverage The use of borrowed funds to increase a project's or a venture's return on cash investment. For leverage to be profitable, the realized rate of return on the investment must be higher than the cost of the money borrowed. Also, the control of large resources with a minimal investment.

leveraged buy out The purchase of assets or stocks of a privately owned company or a public company or a subsidiary of these companies, in which the purchaser uses a significant amount of debt and very little equity capital. This is accomplished by utilizing the purchased assets for collateral and the acquired earnings stream to amortize the debt.

leverage lease A lease in which the financing of equipment is divided into debt and equity portions. The debt portion has a fixed return and is secured by the equipment. The equity portion, the ownership of the equipment, may represent 20 to 25 percent of the original equipment cost. The equity investor receives the tax benefits of equipment ownership, and those benefits may be reflected in the lease rate itself, reducing the lessee's rental payments. The equity investor usually assumes the normal ownership risks. *See* investment tax credit (ITC).

levy A tax or an assessment levied on such things as land.

liability Usually a legal obligation to pay a specific amount at a definite time in return for goods and services received.

liability insurance Insurance covering the policyholder's legal liability for injuries to other persons or damage to their property.

LIBOR (The London Interbank Offered Rate) This rate refers to Euro-dollar deposits traded between banks. There is a different LIBOR rate for each maturity range, reflecting the prevailing yield curve. *See* prime rate.

license fee A charge for issuing a license imposed by a government.

lien A legal right to claim or dispose of property in payment of a debt.

life annuity An insurance contract in which the policyholder receives a certain sum each year for the rest of his life.

life cycle The total phases of a product or business divided into development, growth, maturity, and decline.

life insurance Insurance providing for payment of a specified amount to an estate or a designated beneficiary on the death of the policyholder. The policyholder may borrow against his policy.

limited company A business enterprise or venture in which the liability of each shareholder is limited by the number of shares he has taken, so that he cannot be called on to contribute capital beyond the amount of his shares.

limited guaranty A guaranty limited in the scope of the frequency in which it can be applied to transactions.

limited liability A liability restricted by legal and contractual means.

limited partner A member of a partnership in which one or more partners have a limited liability (to the extent of their financial risk) to partnership creditors. The partnership must have at least one general partner. *See* general partner.

limit of insurance coverage The maximum amount of benefits that an insurer agrees to pay in the event of an acceptable loss.

limit order An order placed with a broker to buy or sell a stated amount of security at a specified price, or at a more favorable price if available. This trading technique is used as a method of specifying the required price for the order.

line A designated authority relationship in an organizational position where one person has responsibility for the activities of another person. This is applicable to both private corporations and government agencies. *See* staff.

line and staff organization A management structure which adds specialists or staff personnel to line organizations. These specialists give advice and make recommendations to line managers.

linear programming A mathematical method used to optimize a goal, to maximize profits, or to minimize costs when there are alternative ways for performing a number of activities and the available resources are limited. *See* dynamic programming.

linear trend In statistical analysis, a trend which, when portrayed on a graph, appears as a straight line.

line of credit An arrangement entered into in advance by which a bank agrees to lend a borrower during some specified period any amount up to the full amount of the line. Sometimes the borrower pays a fee for the potential benefits of the credit facility.

line organization A straight-line relationship between supervisor and subordinate. Usually the system is used in fairly small organizations.

liquid assets Cash, marketable securities, and receivables, not set aside for any specific purpose.

liquidated damages Damages, agreed to in advance, in respect to their amount in the event of a breach of agreement.

liquidation A paid or settled business arrangement which completes or resolves certain claims or liabilities. Also, a closing down of business.

liquidity The ability of an individual, business, or government agency to convert assets quickly into cash without incurring a considerable loss. Short-term, high-quality investments are considered the most marketable items.

liquidity diversification A tool of portfolio management of investing in a variety of maturities of good credit standing so as to reduce the price risk to which investors are exposed when holding long bonds with low ratings.

liquidity risk A financing risk in which the possibility exists that certain monies may not be available at the time they are needed to fund certain assets.

list price The manufacturer's suggested retail price and the price to which the trade discount is applied in order to obtain the retailer's cost price.

Lloyd's Groups of individuals, called syndicates, assuming liability through an underwriter. Each individual independently and personally assumes a proportionate part of the risk accepted by the underwriter. The syndicates usually obtain reinsurance of the insurance in force. Also known as Lloyd's of London, although some Americans are also members.

load In computer sciences, to put data into a register or into storage; to put magnetic tape onto a tape drive or cards into a reader.

In manufacturing, the amount of work a production facility has scheduled ahead.

In mutual funds, the portion of the offering price of shares of open-end investment companies that covers sales commissions and all other costs of distribution. The load is incurred only at the time of purchase. In most cases, there is no charge when the shares are redeemed.

In electric power generation, the amount of power delivered or required at any specified point or points on a system. Load originates primarily at the power-consuming equipment of the customers.

load factor The ratio of the average load in kilowatts supplied during a designated period to the peak or maximum load in kilowatts occurring in that period.

loan The lending of money by a lender to a borrower, to be repaid with a certain amount of interest, usually in the currency of the loan. May be either secured or unsecured, and on a time, demand, or installment basis.

loan certificate Certificates issued by a clearinghouse to the associated banks up to 75 percent of the value of the collateral deposited by the borrowing banks with the clearinghouse.

loan-to-value ratio The ratio between the amount of the mortgage loan and the appraised value of the collateral, expressed as a percentage of the appraised value.

lobbyist A person or organization who attempts to influence legislators to vote in favor of certain legislation.

local advertising Advertising paid for and placed by the retailer at a local rate.

local rate advertising A rate applied to regular advertisers in a newspaper as contrasted with national advertisers.

lockbox system A money-collection system designed to accelerate the flow of funds from the time of customer payment to the time of deposit in the company's bank account.

locking in a rate In a foreign exchange market, establishing the exchange rates at which inflows and outflows of a currency will take place at a given future date.

lockout When employees are locked out of a firm by management until a settlement of the labor dispute is reached.

logistics An analytic approach which determines the optimal transportation, distribution, and warehousing of raw materials, semifinished and finished products, and personnel.

long Signifies ownership of securities. The securities could have been purchased on margin.

long currency position Situation occurring when anticipated inflows of a currency exceed the anticipated outflows of that currency over a given time period.

long-range planning Personal or corporate planning to take into account the future impacts and consequences of past, present, and expected future events.

long-term debt Debt with at least ten years or more of maturity. *See* short-term debt.

long-term financing Refers to the issuance and sale of debt securities with a maturity of more than one year and to that of preferred or common stock for the purpose of raising new capital or refunding outstanding securities. Some consider the one-to-ten-year maturity range as intermediate-term debt.

loss The excess of the cost or depreciated cost of an asset over its selling price.

loss leader A product sold at or below cost in the hope of bringing in customers who will buy other merchandise as well, resulting in net profitable sales.

lump-sum payment A one-time payment, as opposed to payments made in installments. Such payment may be made up front or in the form of a prepayment or acceleration.

M

machine capacity The ratio of the average load on a machine or equipment for the period of time considered to the capacity rating of the machine or equipment.

machine loading In manufacturing, the process of compiling the "load" or quantity of work assigned to each machine for a given period of time. Every job allotted to a machine decreases its capacity for additional work for the time period.

machine rating Limits placed on the operating conditions of a machine, transmission line, apparatus, or device, based on its design characteristics. Such limits as load, voltage, temperature, and frequency may be given in the rating.

macroassembly program A language processor and compiler that accepts words, statements, and phrases to produce machine instructions. The macroassembler permits segmentation of a large program so that portions may be tested separately. It also provides extensive program analysis to aid in debugging.

macroenvironment The totality of major institutions and forces that are external and potentially relevant to the firm.

These issues are usually analyzed by corporate planning departments.

magnetic disk A data-storage device that uses a magnetically coated cylinder.

mail-order advertising A direct-response method of selling goods by receiving and filling orders by mail.

mail-order house An enterprise that markets products by means of catalog orders.

mail payment order An authenticated, nonnegotiable, mail or airmail order issued by a bank authorizing another bank to make a clean payment of a certain sum of money in a specified currency to a certain person or entity.

mainframe The central processor and main memory of a computer system.

maintained markup The difference between the net sales and the gross cost of goods sold.

maintenance expense A cost item which includes labor, materials, and other direct and indirect expenses incurred for preserving the operating efficiency or physical condition of a plant.

malpractice Professional misconduct, lack of skill, or nonperformance of professional duties.

malpractice insurance Coverage for a professional practitioner against liability claims for damages resulting from alleged malpractice in the performance of the insured's services. The coverage is obtained by doctors, lawyers, engineers, and others.

management The process of planning, organizing, directing, and controlling all activities of a business and assuring that all functions are supervised. *See* span of control.

management agreement An agreement among lenders in which one party agrees to coordinate a transaction during its term, including payment processing, legal work, and equipment disposal.

management auditing Reviewing the quality of managers by appraising them as individual managers and also the quality of the total system of managing in an enterprise.

management by exception A management method under which subordinates handle normal assignments and are aware of exceptional events, which they bring to the attention of their superiors.

management by objectives A performance-appraisal plan in which each person sets his own goals as the basis for improving his own performance.

management development An individual-growth program for management personnel, usually at the top or middle level, for the purpose of developing and improving their capabilities; includes planning, organizing, motivating, and controlling the activities of an organization.

management fee A fee received by a person or firm for coordinating a transaction. This concept of payment is applicable in underwriting, leasing, real-estate syndication, and portfolio supervision.

management information systems A process in which data are recorded and processed for operational purposes. The problems are isolated for high-level decision making, and information is fed back to top management to reflect the progress or lack of progress made in achieving major objectives.

management science The use of quantitative methods to provide optimal criteria for allocation decisions concerning people, machines, and other resources in a system involving complex operations. *See* operations research.

management training A system of providing opportunities through various approaches and programs for improving a person's knowledge of the managerial task.

manufacturer's agent A person who represents more than one manufacturer simultaneously and sells only a part of the manufacturer's goods in a designated geographical area.

manufacturer's export representative An export distributor or export commission representative of a domestic manufacturer.

manufacturer's representative An agent who through a commission arranges a sale between the manufacturer and an actual buyer. The function of a manufacturer's representative is similar to that of a broker.

manufacturing order A document or group of documents conveying authority for the manufacture of specified parts or products in specified quantities.

margin The amount deposited by a client with his broker to protect the broker against loss on contracts being carried or to be carried by the broker.

marginal cost The addition to the total cost of one extra unit of output. Due to economy of scale, most manufacturing industries benefit from reductions in unit cost as their volume of output increases until plant capacity is reached. *See* incremental cost.

marginal tax rate The combined federal, state, and local tax rate that would have to be paid on any additional dollars of taxable income earned.

margin call The amount paid by the customer when he uses his broker's credit to buy a stock and other securities. Under Federal Reserve regulations, the initial margin required in the past years has ranged from 50 percent of the purchase price all the way to 100 percent. The lending rate on margin is usually the prime rate plus a specified percentage of that rate.

markdown A reduction in the original selling price taken to move merchandise.

market The group of all actual and potential buyers of a product. The procedures for bidding, the methods of trading, and the settlement procedures have to be agreed to by market participants for an orderly functioning of the group.

marketable securities Negotiable stocks, bonds, and U.S. Treasury securities carried as a current asset and representing investments of surplus cash.

market approach to value The value of a product or an asset such as real estate is estimated by the actual prices paid in market transactions.

market demand The total volume of a particular item purchased by a consumer group.

market development A company's ability to seek increased sales by taking its current products into new markets.

market forecast Refers to the expected level of market demand for the expected level of business marketing effort.

marketing The function of a company in directing products from manufacturer to final consumer, including advertising, credit financing, packaging, transporting, market research, and warehousing.

marketing channel The course taken by goods and products from producer to consumer. *See* channel of distribution.

marketing concept A business objective of orienting the products and services of a company to meet the requirements of the marketplace.

marketing management The analysis, planning, implementation, and control of programs.

marketing mix The combination of objectives of a firm that selects a marketing approach so that the selected target markets are penetrated in an optimal fashion.

marketing strategy A business approach by which the business unit intends to achieve its marketing objectives through the determination of target markets, marketing mix, and marketing expenditure level.

market penetration The ability of a firm to advance its products or services into a particular marketplace or market segment.

market potential The total sales of a product that a market is estimated to be able to absorb during a given period.

market price The last reported price at which a stock, bond, or other assets changed hands or were reported sold.

market profile Socioeconomic description of persons in a given product market.

market research The use of empirical and statistical information concerning consumers or purchasers to determine purchasers' behavior and perception of the various characteristics of products.

market segmentation The division of a market into distinct groups and subgroups of buyers who might merit separate products or marketing mixes.

market share A product's sales as a percentage of all sales of similar products, or the share of a company's products in an industry.

market skimming Exploiting only the prime market segment of a product's or a company's marketplace which is either the most profitable, the least costly to reach, or requires the least amount of available resources.

mass marketing A process of mass producing and mass selling of a product, and merchandising the goods to a very large segment of the population.

mass media advertising The use of any media whose audience consists of the general population, such as radio, newspaper, or television advertising.

mass medium An advertising medium widely accepted by all types of people.

mass production Large-scale production employing standardized parts and specialized labor. *See* production.

master lease A lease line of credit or a financing arrangement that allows a lessee to add property under the same basic terms and conditions without negotiating a new lease contract.

materiality The relative importance of an item or event measured against other sets of circumstances.

materials handling A production-distribution function of developing the most efficient unit loads, improving the use of floor and cubic space, and selecting the handling equipment.

materials management A function concerned with the movement of materials, production control, inventory control, traffic, storage, materials handling, purchasing, and other similarly related activities.

matrix A mathematical coding network having height, width, and sometimes depth, into which collections of data may be stored and processed.

matrix management A management style in which multiple functions are coordinated by a supervisor.

matrix organization A grid organization used to coordinate product development, manufacturing, and marketing, in which more than one department has a role.

maturity The date at which an obligation, such as a bond or a mortgage, becomes due.

maximum stock The minimum stock available at all times plus the amount of stock that might be sold during the period of time elapsing before the next reorder point. *See* fluctuation inventory.

mean Arithmetic mean is the sum of the values of the items divided by the number of items; geometric mean is a term between the first and last terms of a geometric progression.

mechanic's lien The claim of a worker or contractor on a building or its land to protect against loss of pay for work performed or loss of materials used in the construction of that building or improvements.

median The median of a group of *n* numbers is the middle number of the group if *n* is odd, and it is the mean of the two middle numbers if *n* is even.

mediation The third party in a labor-management dispute, the mediator, can make specific recommendations for the settlement of the dispute.

Medicaid A social-benefit program of hospital and medical insurance for low-income and poor people, financed by a mix of federal, state, and local funds.

medical payments insurance An insurance coverage which provides for payment, without regard for liability, of medical and similar expenses resulting from a peril insured by the policy.

member bank A commercial bank that is a member of the Federal Reserve System. All national banks are automatically members of the System. State banks may be admitted. By law, member banks must hold reserves (their own vault cash and deposits with their Federal Reserve Banks) that are equal to a percentage of their customers' deposits. *See* Board of Governors of the Federal Reserve System.

memorandum of understanding A written document detailing the points upon which two or more parties are agreed. *See* verbal agreement.

merchandise Finished goods bought by a retailer and held in inventory for resale.

merchandising Those marketing functions involved with presenting and selling goods, including advertising, displaying, promoting, and direct selling.

merchant bank A term generally used in Europe to describe a financial institution engaged both in investment banking and commercial banking activities involving the selling of securities and accepting deposits among other services. *See* investment banker.

merchant middlemen Business firms, such as wholesalers, distributors, and retailers, that buy, take title to, and resell merchandise.

merger The fusion of two or more unrelated businesses into a single legal entity. The merger usually takes place for stock and cash. *See* acquisition.

merit increase A voluntary pay increase to an individual employee because of the quality of his work or improved efficiency, or as a reward for increased production, improvement in attitude, or quality of performance.

message A segment of information whose beginning and end are defined or implied, such as communication of information or advice from a source to one or more destinations in suitable language or code.

methods analysis An industrial engineering approach to various techniques and methods for increasing production through the proper and economic use of motion, thereby saving time either by the organization of work or by the breaking down of the process so that the job can be performed more efficiently. *See* value analysis.

methods-time measurement In manufacturing procedures, a technique for acquiring data that may apply to all classes of work involving manual motions.

microelectronic device A product made up of interconnected transistors, resistors, capacitors, and similar components. Silicon is the primary material for microelectronic circuits. *See* Silicon Valley.

microfilm Photographic film used in a machine which photographs various records and documents for easy storage and retrieval.

middleman A businessman who buys directly from the manufacturer and then sells to the consumer. He makes his living by "marking up" the wholesale price he paid the manufacturer and charging the consumer the higher retail price. The middleman is usually paid a flat fee or a percentage of the deal. *See* facilitators.

middle management A group of company employees whose position is between top management and the front-line supervisors. The middle manager carries out the programs and policies of the senior executives, and at the same time coordinates those functions through the field offices and front-line junior managers.

middle-of-the-road style A management style which balances the need to get the work done with maintaining a satisfactory level of morale among the employees.

milestone budgeting A planning technique which breaks down a program or project into identifiable and controllable pieces or elements.

military-industrial complex An informal network of relationships between the U.S. Department of Defense and suppliers of equipment for the military.

minicomputer A small, programmable, general-purpose computer often used for dedicated application or for distributed processing. *See* personal computer.

minimum charge The basic rate a person is charged for the use of a utility, such as a telephone or electricity, whether or not the utility is used.

minimum stock Minimum stock = reserve (weeks) + delivery period (weeks). By avoiding an out-of-stock condition, a firm could maintain a continuous operation.

minimum wage laws A standard established by federal law requiring an hourly minimum payment to workers. *See* piece wages.

min/max inventory system An industrial procedure for stock replenishment that establishes points at which the minimum quantity on hand indicates the need to reorder so as to return the quantity to the maximum level.

Minority Enterprise Small Business Investment Company (MESBIC) Government-sponsored venture-capital companies which serve only those small businesses that are owned by a minority group, a minority-group individual, or other socially and economically disadvantaged Americans.

minority interest Stock in a subsidiary company allocable to those owners who are not part of the controlling interest.

misbranding False or misleading labeling, which may be used by promoters who wish to profit from the popularity of a well-known product.

model A representation of a process or system (financial, governmental, industrial, or managerial) that attempts to relate the most important variables in the system in such a way that analysis of the model leads to insights into the system. Frequently, the model is used to anticipate the result of some particular strategy in the real system.

modified accrual basis The basis of accounting under which expenditures other than accrued interest on general long-term debt are recorded at the time liabilities are incurred and revenues are recorded when received in cash, except for material and/or available revenues, which should be accrued to reflect properly the taxes levied and the revenues earned.

modified closed shop Any contract that requires a closed shop but exempts certain groups of employees from the union membership requirement, such as present employees who are not members or employees who have been with the company for a minimum period of time.

modified union shop Any union-shop agreement which deviates from the general standard requiring that all employees become members of the union after a certain period of time following employment. *See* union shop.

module In data processing, an interchangeable, usually plug-in assembly or subassembly of components.

money market The market in which short-term debt instruments, such as U.S. Treasury bills, commercial paper, and bankers' acceptances, are issued and traded.

money market center banks Usually refers to the top ten to fifteen banks in the United States, headquartered in New York, Chicago, San Francisco, or Los Angeles. These banks are trend setters for the establishment of the prime rate and other financial services.

money market funds Short-term investment vehicles, oriented primarily to individuals who wish to take advantage of high short-term rates. The funds invest their assets into high-yielding securities, such as commercial paper, bankers' acceptances, and treasury bills. Some funds provide checking accounts for their investors.

money order An order for the payment of money, as issued by one post office or bank to another post office or bank.

money supply definitions used by the Federal Reserve System The most important are: M1-A = currency + demand deposits; M1-B = M1-A + other checkable deposits. These figures are usually issued at the end of the business week.

Monte Carlo simulation A trial-and-error method in which the models are based on random or stochastic processes.

These methods of simulation are used when experimentation is either impossible or too expensive.

monopoly A nearly complete control of a commodity, product, labor supply, or service in a particular market. *See* cartel.

moratorium of repayment A period during which a creditor grants a borrower the right to delay the fulfillment of an obligation.

mortgage A claim or security interest given by the borrower (mortgagor) to the lender (mortgagee) against the borrower's property in return for a loan. *See* construction loan.

mortgage-backed securities An investment security structured as a bond, representing an undivided interest in a pool of mortgages or trust deeds. Income from the underlying mortgage is used to pay off the securities. *See* pass-through security.

mortgage banker Individuals or firms which act as mortgage originators and serve as local representatives of regional or national institutional lenders.

mortgage banking The packaging of mortgage loans secured by real property to be sold to a permanent investor (a private lender or a government agency) with servicing (for a fee) retained for the life of the loan. The origination, sale, and servicing of mortgage loans is also a mortgage banking function.

mortgage discount The difference between the principal amount of a mortgage and the amount it actually sells for. Sometimes called points, loan brokerage fee, or new loan fee. The discount is computed on the amount of the loan, not the sale price.

mortgagee A creditor to whom property is conveyed as security for a loan made by a person or firm.

mortgage insurance A type of term life insurance often bought by mortgagors. The amount of coverage decreases as the mortgage balance declines. In the event that the borrower dies while the policy is in force, the debt is automatically satisfied by insurance proceeds.

mortgage portfolio The aggregate of mortgage loans held by an investor and serviced by a mortgage banker or by the investor.

mortgage revenue bonds Tax-exempt bonds issued by state and local governments to provide low-interest-rate loans for single and multifamily housing developments and projects.

mortgage, second A financial instrument which, in terms of security, ranks subordinate to the first mortgage. The second mortgage is usually for a smaller amount and a shorter term than the first mortgage.

mortgagor One who borrows money, giving as security a mortgage or deed of trust on real property.

motion study An analysis of the movements of machinery and materials as they relate to the actual motion of the individual worker. This is done so that unnecessary and uneconomical movements can be eliminated and a proper sequence arranged to standardize performance, obtain greater productivity, and create the least-waste method of production.

motive A physiological and psychological need which a person strives to satisfy in the shortest possible time period.

moving average A statistical measure which relates to the general direction of a series rather than to a specific point in the data base under study.

multinational corporation A corporation, conducting business in two or more countries, whose foreign and domestic interests are interlocked in an international operation.

multinational marketing A company which is simultaneously marketing its products and services in more than one country.

multiperil policy A package policy which provides coverage against several different perils.

multiple access Pertains to a system in which input and output may be dispatched or received at more than one geographic location, or with more than one device at a single location. *See* random access.

multiple-line policy A multiperil policy which combines both property and liability coverages.

municipal bond A security issued by a state government, county, city, or other special district, or by a public authority or nonprofit corporation. Bonds are usually one to forty years in maturity and carry coupons, which are redeemed for the payment of interest. Interest income from the bonds is exempt from federal income taxation. In most cases, investors residing in the state in which the bonds are issued are also exempt from taxes of that state. *See* exempt securities.

municipal corporation An entity established pursuant to state authorization for the purpose of providing governmental services and regulations for its inhabitants. A municipal corporation has defined boundaries and a population, and is usually organized with the consent of its residents. It may sue and be sued. Cities and towns are examples of municipal corporations.

municipally owned electric system An electric utility system owned and/or operated by a municipality engaged in serving residential, commercial, and/or industrial customers, usually within the boundaries of the municipality. *See* investor-owned electric utilities.

mutual fund An open-end investment company, which sells its shares to the public and is ready to buy them back in the future. *See* investment company.

mutual savings bank A thrift institution owned by the depositors. The assets of the bank are invested in high-yielding obligations and mortgages. Dividends from these investments are distributed to depositors after deductions for expenses and reserves.

N

naked option An option sold on stock that the writer of the option does not own; also known as uncovered option.

national advertising plan A regional or geographic media campaign whose objective is to reduce the cost of advertising to the lowest cost per thousand.

National Association of Securities Dealers Automated Quotations System (NASDAQ) A computerized communications system serving the over-the-counter market. There are three levels of service available: Level one is used largely by registered representatives, level two by retail traders, and level three by market makers.

national banks Banks chartered by the federal government and regulated by the Comptroller of the Currency and the Federal Deposit Insurance Corporation. Most national banks are also members of the Federal Reserve System.

national brand A brand name owned by a manufacturer. Known also as manufacturer's brand.

National Labor Relations Board (N.L.R.B.) A federal agency, established in 1935 for the purpose of handling disputes between management and labor.

natural monopolies A limited number of industries, such as utilities and railroads, enjoy some form of natural monopoly. Most of these companies are highly regulated by federal or state governmental agencies.

negative carry The net cost incurred when the cost of financing a security position exceeds the yield on the securities being financed.

negative cash flow A financial situation when cash expenditures of an income-producing project are in excess of the cash receipts from the project.

negotiable certificates of deposit Certificates issued by commercial banks under applicable Federal Reserve regulations, with an interest rate either fixed for a period of time or variable with respect to some financial index or government security.

negotiable instrument Under the Uniform Commercial Code, an instrument that meets certain legal requirements and can be transferred by endorsement or delivery.

negotiated underwriting A financing arrangement when the terms of an offering are determined by negotiation between the issuer and the underwriter rather than through competitive bidding by underwriting groups. The price paid for the securities reflects market conditions at the time of the sale. *See* competitive bidding.

negotiations The process of settling or arranging the terms and conditions of a bargain, sale, or other business transaction. These are done through meetings, discussions, and other forms of deliberation.

net assets The excess of the book value of the assets of an accounting unit over its liabilities.

net current assets Working capital.

net exchange position A net asset or liability position in a specific currency. Also referred to as a net long or a net short position.

net income The excess of all revenues for a period of time over all the expenses of that period.

net lease A financing method in which the rentals are payable net to the lessor. All costs in connection with the use of the equipment are to be paid by the lessee and are not a part of the rental. These include taxes, insurance, and maintenance, which are paid directly by the lessee. Most capital leases and direct-financing leases are net leases.

net mortgage yield That part of the gross yield which remains after the deductions of all costs, such as servicing, pool insurance, and any reserves for losses.

net period The date beyond the cash discount date that the retailer is allowed to make full payment of the invoice. If no cash discount is allowed, the period is assumed to be thirty days.

net present value Discounted value of all cash inflows and outflows of a project.

net price This represents the price the buyer must pay for the merchandise and is the retailer's cost price.

net terms This indicates that the manufacturer is not allowing a cash discount and that the invoice amount will be due in full at the expiration of the net period.

network Computer linkages covering geographically separate areas. In human systems, the interrelationship between organizations, groups, and persons with similar interests and functions.

net worth The value of all assets, including cash, less total liabilities. It is often used as a guideline to indicate credit worthiness and financial strength.

new-issues market The formal or over-the-counter markets in which a new issue of securities is first sold to investors.

new money In a U.S. Treasury refunding, the amount by which the par value of the securities offered exceeds the amount maturing at that time.

New York Stock Exchange A voluntary association of members who execute stock and bond trades mostly on the floor of the Stock Exchange. The Exchange, in cooperation with the National Association of Securities Dealers, offers an exam for registered representatives who are customers' brokers handling retail buyers and sellers. Specialists on the floor of the Exchange are responsible for maintaining an orderly market for the trading of securities.

New York Stock Exchange Common Stock Index A composite index covering price movements of all common stocks listed on the Big Board.

no-fault automobile insurance A form of coverage by which a person's financial losses resulting from an automobile accident, such as medical and hospital expenses and loss of income, are paid by his own insurance company without regard to fault.

nominal lease A leveraged lease in which the lessor will recover his investment from tax benefits, offset rents against debt payments, and never receive a rent payment.

nominal lessor A lessor under a nominal lease.

nominal partner A person who lends his name to a business firm but who is not actually a partner.

noncompetitive bid The average price of an accepted bid at a U.S. Treasury auction, which is submitted on a competitive basis and establishes the price for noncompetitive tenders.

nondurable goods Tangible goods, which cannot be expected to last for a relatively long time even though used infrequently. *See* durable goods.

nonpayout lease A lease which does not, over the initial term of the lease, generate enough cash flow to return all, or substantially all, of the lessor's investment and costs.

nonrecourse debt financing A financing technique in which the property or equipment is the only source of security to the lender, and the borrower does not pledge any additional collateral or guarantee to strengthen the financing. *See* recourse debt financing.

no-strike clause A clause in a contract whereby a union agrees it will not strike during the life of the contract.

notary public A public officer authorized by a state to authenticate contracts, take affidavits, and take depositions.

nuclear energy The energy liberated by a nuclear reaction (fission or fusion) or by radioactive decay.

numeraire In international corporate finance, this refers to the currency chosen by a firm as a reference against which all other currency cash flows are measured.

O

objective function The goal or function to be optimized in a business enterprise. In most cases, costs are minimized while profits are maximized, subject to outside constraints.

obsolescence The loss of product or asset value resulting from a model or style change or a technological development.

occupancy rate The ratio of apartment units or offices rented as compared with the total number contained within the building; or the ratio of leases to total space, expressed as a percentage.

off budget Transactions that have been excluded from the budget totals under provisions of law, e.g., the Federal Financing Bank. Off-budget transactions are not included in either the budget authority or outlay totals, but are presented in a separate part of the budget appendix and as memorandum items in various budgetary tables.

offer The price at which a seller of securities is ready to sell. *See* bid.

offering A primary stock offering relates to the original sale of a company's stock, while a secondary offering refers to the resale of stock sometime after its initial offering.

off-line system In data processing, a system and its peripheral devices in which the operation of the peripheral equipment is not under the control of the central processing unit, but requires human supervision.

off-peak energy Electric energy supplied during periods of relative low system demands, as specified by the supplier.

oligopoly An industry in which a very small number of companies dominate the market and offer relatively identical products at an oligopolistic price.

on account A purchase or sale in which payment is expected sometime after delivery. A current sale based on credit terms.

on consignment The goods of one manufacturer or distributor delivered to another for sale may be returned if the items are unsold. In this type of transaction, the manufacturer takes the risk of production and market acceptance of his products.

one-sided market A market in which the bid, or the asked, is quoted. Also known as a one-way market.

one-time rate The rate paid by an advertiser who uses less space than is necessary to earn a discount, when such discounts are offered.

on-line processing A technique in which transactions are processed as soon as they are received rather than being stored in a file.

on-the-job-training An educational program which utilizes the actual job or work site as the place at which an individual receives instruction while at the same time engaging in productive work.

open account Any account which is not closed out.

open-end agreement A settlement between employer and injured employee in a workmen's compensation case in which the payments for disability from injuries continue as long as the employee is unable to work.

open-end contract An understanding in which the exact amount of goods or services to be bought is not specified, but the provider agrees to deliver as many goods or services as the purchaser will require to meet his needs.

open-ended system Any process or system that has no inherent restriction. The system presents no boundaries or constraining parameters that could limit action.

open-end investment trust A fund in which the trustees and fiduciaries have the discretion to buy and sell securities for the benefit of the trust.

open-end mortgage A mortgage with a provision that the outstanding loan amount may be increased upon mutual agreement of the lender and the borrower.

open-end question In market research, a question that the respondent is free to answer in his or her own words. *See* closed-end question.

open repurchase agreement A repurchase agreement with no definite expiration rate, but with an adjustable interest rate. *See* repurchase agreement.

open shop A company in which workers have the right to decide if they desire to become members of the union. *See* closed shop.

operating budget A detailed projection of all current income and expenses for a given period rather than an account of capital items.

operating expenses Expenses incurred during the ordinary activities of an enterprise.

operating lease A transaction in which the lessor provides, or is responsible for, the maintenance in connection with the agreement.

operating leverage A business structure of a company whose costs are largely fixed, even under different levels of sales. If sales increase even slightly above break even, a relatively large profit could result. Likewise, if sales decrease, a significant loss could occur.

operating ratio The ratio, in percentage, of the operating expenses to the operating revenues.

operating statement An income statement summarizing the revenues, expenses, and income of any specific operating entity, such as a profit center, a department, a subsidiary, or an entire company.

operational audit A periodic and independent appraisal by a staff of internal auditors of the accounting, financial, and other operations of an enterprise.

operations research The development and application of quantitative techniques and mathematical models to the solution of problems faced by managers of public and private organizations. The objective of these models is to find optimal solutions, given certain aims and goals of the enterprise. *See* management science.

opportunity costs The return on human and financial capital that could have resulted had the capital been used for some purpose other than its present use. Also refers to the best alternative use of the capital.

optimization A method of arriving at the most desirable set of conditions based on a set of criteria or constraints. Usually, this is done through mathematical methods employing large amounts of data, which are analyzed through the use of high-speed computers.

optimization, linear The process for locating the maximum, minimum, or other optimum value or values of a function of variables which are themselves subject to mathematically linear constraints and inequalities.

optimization, nonlinear The process used for locating the maximum, minimum, or other optimum value or values of a function of variables which are nonlinear constraints and inequalities.

option A contractual right to buy something during a specified period of time at a specified price. Payment is generally required for such an option. *See* call; put.

oral contract A spoken contract, which is a gentlemen's agreement. In most cases, the oral understanding is not legally binding until it is reduced to written form.

ordinary income Income subject to normal taxation rates, as distinct from income subject to special tax treatment (such as capital gains). It is the income that is derived from a company's or from a person's main business and employment.

organization A network of relationships, procedures, habits, and patterns which form the elements required for the functioning of a public or private enterprise.

organizational buying The decision-making process by which formal organizations establish the need for purchased products and services, and for identifying, evaluating, and choosing among alternative brands and suppliers.

organizational chart The formal structural outline of the company.

organizational development A planned process for changing a business system. Its two essential phases are diagnosis and intervention. The factors studied for bringing about change include: behavior problems, attitudes, motives, and values of managers and subordinates in an enterprise.

organization costs The costs incurred in planning and establishing an entity.

organization manual A handbook given to employees containing essential information on company policies and procedures. The actual policies and procedures of the company may be set through informal communications and directives rather than by published manual.

organization structure The formal and informal framework which shows the authority and responsibility relationships among people, the communication channels, the relationship of each part of the company to the others, and the interrelationship between the company and its subsidiaries.

outlays The amount of checks issued, the interest accrued on most public debts, or other payments, net of refunds and reimbursements. Total budget outlays consist of the sum of the outlays from appropriations and funds included in the unified budget, less offsetting receipts.

out-of-pocket expenses Expenses paid by persons in connection with the normal conduct of business. Travel, lodging, and food are included in this class of expenses.

output Data that have been processed and are available for detailed analysis by decision makers.

outright forward rate An exchange rate calculated in terms of the amount of one currency required to buy a unit of another currency.

outstanding Unpaid or uncollected bills or accounts receivable. When said of stock, it means the quantity of shares issued less treasury stock.

overabsorption A credit-balance condition which develops when more overhead costs are applied to a product than are incurred.

overall capitalization rate The relationship between net operating income and the total project cost.

overhead costs Any cost of doing business not specifically associated with the production of identifiable goods and services.

overlapping debt The proportionate share of the debts of local governmental units, located wholly or in part within the limits of the reporting government, which must be borne by the property within each governmental unit.

overnight delivery risk Due to time-zone differences, the risk borne by buyers and sellers settling a transaction in a time zone other than the one in which a security was bought.

overrun The quantity received from a manufacturer or a vendor that is in excess of the original order.

Overseas Private Investment Corporation An agency of the U.S. Treasury, its objective is to stimulate and facilitate United States private equity and loan investments in friendly developing countries. The Corporation offers the following programs: investment insurance, guarantees, direct loans, preinvestment information, counseling, and cost sharing. The risks covered are: inconvertibility of profits or repatriation of the original investment, loss of investment due to expropriation or confiscation by the foreign government, and damage to property resulting from war, revolution, or insurrection. *See* Export-Import Bank.

over-the-counter (OTC) market A telephone-based market for securities not listed on any U.S. stock exchange which are traded nationally and internationally directly between buyers and sellers, usually through dealers.

owners' equity Assets minus liabilities or net worth.

ownership The rights to use and enjoy property, including the right to transfer it to others.

owner-trustee A financial institution which holds title to the equipment for the benefit of the equity participants. It also takes on the normal trustee duties required for a multiparty secured transaction.

P

pacer A worker used by a company to set the pace for other workers in a factory, or to establish piecework rates.

package advertising In broadcast advertising, a combination of time units sold as a single offering at a set price.

package freight Materials and products shipped in less-than-carload lots and billed by the piece.

paid-in capital The total amount of cash, property, and services invested by the owners or stockholders in a business. It represents the legal capital of a corporation and normally may not be reduced except upon liquidation or other appropriate legal action.

paid-in surplus The capital and other assets invested in a business by the owners or stockholders over and above the paid-in capital. It is usually the difference between the issuing price and the par value of a corporation's outstanding common stock. *See* capital surplus.

paper profit An unrealized profit on a security or an asset still held. Paper profits are turned into real profits only when the security or asset is sold.

par The principal amount of a mortgage or bond with no premium or discount. The price of 100 percent. *See* discount.

parameter A variable that is given a constant value for a specific analytic or decision-making purpose.

parent company A company owning more than 50 percent of the shares of another company, called the subsidiary. The parent may also be a holding company.

parity A ratio between prices received by farmers and prices paid to them in some prior base period.

participation loan A loan made by a consortium of banks, sometimes referred to as a syndicated loan. The purpose of the syndication is to spread the risk inherent in the loan. Also, the legal lending limits of banks may require them to form joint ventures with other banks.

participatory leadership A management approach in which the senior executive advises and consults on major decisions. He nevertheless delegates the final decisions to his associates and subordinates.

partnership A contractual arrangement between individuals to share resources and operations in a jointly run business. They also share in the legal liability of the business.

partnership, limited A partnership involving one or more general partners that involves a financial agreement under which a contributor to the partnership is liable, if the company should fail, only for the sum of money he invested, and benefits only to the extent of his financial contribution.

par value The face amount of a security.

passbook loan A loan secured by the borrower's savings account balance. The passbook and a withdrawal agreement are pledged to and left with the bank or savings and loan association as collateral.

pass-through security A financial instrument, usually a bond, whose security is the mortgage payment passed through to the investor from the underlying pool of mortgages deposited with the trustee. *See* mortgage-backed securities.

patent Exclusive rights granted by the government to an inventor for a period of time to enjoy the results of his invention.

patent pending A designation describing the legal status of a patent application while a search is conducted by the U.S. Patent Office as to the patentability of the invention.

payable Unpaid, but not necessarily due or past due.

pay-as-you-go basis The financial policy of a governmental unit which finances all of its capital outlays from current revenues rather than by borrowing. A governmental unit which pays for some improvements from current revenues and for others by borrowing is said to be on a partial or modified pay-as-you-go basis.

payback period The amount of time that must elapse before the revenue inflows from a project equal the revenue outflows.

pay down An authorization by the borrower to pay back, to the bank, a portion of his loan.

payout After-tax earnings per share, which are paid to stockholders in the form of dividends.

payout ratio The ratio of a company's earnings paid to stockholders as dividends to the earnings obtained within a specific accounting period.

payroll taxes Taxes levied on salaries and wages. The employer pays a portion and deducts part of the employee's wages for the other portion.

peaking Generating units or stations, which are available to assist in meeting that portion of the peak load which is above the base load.

penny stocks In securities trading, a low-priced issue of new companies that is speculative and sells for less than a dollar a share. Many of the penny stocks are marketed through Denver-based security dealers, known generally as the Denver Stock Exchange. *See* blue-chip stock.

pension A regular payment made to a retired employee who has met the pension requirements of the company.

pension fund A fund established to cover the costs of the particular pension plan established, and maintained by an employer under sound actuarial standards to provide retirement payments of specific amounts to employees over the period of their retirement.

pension plan A provision of an employer's contract with employees for paying retirement annuities. *See* Keogh plan.

percentage of completion method An accounting practice of recording revenues and expenditures relative to the percentage of costs expended or monies received in relation to the total to be allocated for a project.

perception The process by which an individual selects, organizes, and interprets information in order to create a meaningful picture of his environment.

performance bond A bond used to guarantee performance of a specified contract, such as the completion of construction or off-site improvements. *See* surety.

performance standards The level and quality of output expected of workers. *See* surety.

period expense A periodic expense charged to an operation rather than counted as an asset.

periodic inventory valuation A method of recording inventory that uses data on beginning, additions to, and ending inventory in order to find the cost of withdrawals from inventory.

permanent investor One who provides long-term financing. Usually these investors are insurance companies, pension funds, and bond funds.

permanent loan A long-term or mortgage loan that is generally amortized over more than seven to ten years. *See* interim financing.

perpetual annuity Regular payments which continue for an unlimited period of time, including after the death of the beneficiary.

perpetual inventory An inventory-control system which maintains a running account of materials and parts on hand.

perpetuity An annuity whose payments last forever, and may be interrupted only by war or other very significant developments.

personal assets Individual property such as goods, real estate, securities, jewelry, furniture, houses, apartment houses, insurance policies, and other items.

personal computer A low-cost computer based on tiny microcomputer chips and thus portable, personally controllable, and easily used. There are several user categories: home, hobbyist, professional, business, very small business, appliance, and others. *See* minicomputer.

personal consumption expenditures Goods and services purchased by individuals and nonprofit institutions, and the value of food, clothing, rental of dwellings, and financial services received in kind by individuals. All private purchases of dwellings are classified as gross private domestic investments.

personal liability Lenders may require a personal guaranty on a loan in addition to the pledged collateral, such as equipment or real estate.

personal property Classified as anything which is subject to ownership, such as jewelry, clothing, money, securities, and tools.

personnel administration An administrative program used to implement the human-resources policies of a corporation with the aim of setting wage standards and creating a better utilization of the employees.

personnel policy The formal and informal standards of a corporation with respect to hiring, promotion, and termination of employment.

personnel relations The activities of the management in communicating with individual employees so as to improve their utilization within the organization.

petrodollar Money invested by oil-producing countries through international banks, usually headquartered in London.

petty cash An office management practice of setting aside small sums of money to cover minor expenses.

physical distribution The tasks involved in planning and implementing the physical flows of materials and final goods from the points of origin to points of use or consumption.

picketing During a labor conflict, the practice of workers marching at the entrance to a firm to protest some management practice.

piece rate Payment to workers on the basis of the number of acceptable units of output produced. In most cases, the federal and state minimum hourly pay requirements must also be met.

piece wages Total wages paid on the basis of the number of units produced. *See* minimum wage laws.

piggyback The transportation system of combining motor and rail transportation services. *See* containerization.

pilot production A sample run of a new product to test the validity of its design and documentation and evaluate production methods. Market testing is usually conducted at this state of product development.

planned obsolescence A manufacturing and marketing concept that incorporates into the original production a plan which defines the life of a product. Certain stylistic or functional parameters are incorporated in the item that would require the purchase of a new product prior to the end of the normal useful life of the original item.

planning The management function of formulating in advance the directions, strategies, programs, and procedures a firm is to follow to reach its most optimal objectives.

planning process A rational approach to accomplishing an objective vis-à-vis evaluating alternatives in the light of goals sought and within available manpower, financial, and time resources.

plant assets Buildings, machinery, and land.

pledged asset An asset that has been placed in trust or given as collateral for an obligation, loan, or mortgage. Also known as "hypothecated asset." *See* hypothecate.

point In mortgage finance, a point is equal to 1 percent of the principal amount of an investment. In the United States securities market, one point is equivalent to one dollar.

pooling-of-interests method A common method of accounting for a merger of two companies in which each beneficial interest continues in a new or modified organization as to its book value, and its relative interest in paid-in capital and earned surplus substantially unchanged.

portfolio A group of investment securities held by an individual or institution and managed by them or by outside advisors. It generally denotes a mixture of bonds, preferred stocks, and common stocks of many companies.

positioning A marketing effort to develop and position products to reach target markets and, at the same time, maximize profits against other brands.

postaudit An audit which follows a normal audit of a transaction or an agency.

power-factor adjustment clause A clause in an electric rate schedule that provides for an adjustment in the billing if the customer's power factor varies from a specified percentage or range of percentages.

power pool A power pool is two or more interconnected electric systems planned and operated to supply power in the most reliable and economical manner for their combined load requirements and maintenance program.

preaudit A financial examination of a transaction or an agency to determine the propriety of the activities which have taken place.

preemptive right A privilege given to a stockholder to subscribe to a pro-rata share of any new capital stock a corporation is to issue.

preferred position A special location for advertisements placed in the print media for which additional fees are charged.

preferred stock The class of stock which has a claim prior to common stock on the earnings of a corporation and on its assets in the event of liquidation. *See* common stock.

premium The amount by which the price of a security or other asset exceeds its par or market value. Also, the price of an option or contract, as in an insurance policy. In advertising, a gift or inducement given to a purchaser as an incentive to buy the product.

premium bond Bond selling above par. *See* discount bond.

prepaid expense An expenditure that leads to a deferred charge.

prepayment A partial or full payment made ahead of the scheduled payment date.

prepayment fee An amount paid to a lender for the privilege of prepaying an obligation. Also known as a prepayment penalty or reinvestment fee.

prepayment privilege The right given to a borrower to pay all or part of a debt prior to its maturity.

present value The value today of an amount to be received in the future, discounted at some interest rate.

President's budget The budget for a particular fiscal year transmitted to the U.S. Congress by the President in accordance with the Budget and Accounting Act of 1921, as amended. Some elements of the budget, such as the estimates for the legislative branch and the judiciary, are required to be included without review by the Office of Management and Budget or approval by the President.

price earnings (p/e) ratio The price of a stock divided by its earnings per share.

price fixing An unlawful conspiracy among producers and/or distributors to fix the price of a product at a specified level and thereby limiting competition in the marketplace.

price leader A product or service that is priced below its normal markup or even below cost. It is used to attract customers in the hope that they will buy other things at normal markups.

price level accounting An accounting method of adjusting corporate assets to reflect inflationary factors and price changes in the economy.

price level adjusted mortgage (PLAM) The interest rate is fixed, but the outstanding balance and monthly payments change according to the changes in some price index.

price-taking market A market where each seller must charge the going price.

price variance A rate change resulting from a change in the price of materials or labor.

pricing strategy The price estimates, both present and future, which a product is most likely to carry in the marketplace, taking into account the price of competing products, cost of production, distribution, and other factors.

primary data Original data collected from the source. Generally used in market research. *See* secondary data.

primary service area A geographic area where a radio or television station delivers its signals in the clearest and steadiest fashion.

primary storage The memory of a computer, in which instructions and data being worked upon are contained.

prime advertising rate The television and radio rate for the times when broadcasts reach the largest audiences.

prime rate The rate for loans charged by commercial banks to their most preferred customers. *See* LIBOR.

prime time The three-hour period from 8:00 to 11:00 P.M. (in the Eastern Standard Time zone) when the target number of audiences are watching television.

principal The face value of a security. Also, the person who is mainly responsible for an obligation or a commitment.

prior-period adjustment A change which may be made retroactively to an accounting statement, reflecting significant prior events which were not recorded at the time in which they occurred.

private brand A brand name owned by a middleman, such as a distributor.

private placement The selling of stock or debt obligations to a limited number of private investors and institutional buyers by an issuing company or governmental entity, or by an investment banking firm, but not by public offering. *See* public offering.

procedures Chronological sequences of required actions, detailing the exact manner in which an activity must be carried out.

proceeds Funds received from the disposition of assets or from the sale of securities.

process heat Heat used for the industrial process of a plant and not the housekeeping chores, such as space heating.

process time The time during which the material is being changed, whether it is a machining operation or a hand assembly.

product Anything that has value and can be sold in a market. The product can be an object, a service, an organization, a song, or an idea.

product concept A business assumption that consumers will favor those products that offer the most quality for the price, and therefore the organization should devote its energy to improving quality.

product development A concerted effort by a company to further the development of existing products and create new markets by the introduction of new concepts not yet marketed by the company's competitors.

product differentiation The attempt by producers, advertisers, or consumers to distinguish between nearly similar products.

product image The perception of the product or service by the consumer will determine in great part the market acceptance of the item.

production All functions connected with shaping virgin products to final finished goods. *See* mass production.

production basis accounting An accounting system used to recognize sales from highly liquid products, such as gold, which are assumed to sell immediately at current market prices.

production control A function which monitors the orderly flow of work in manufacturing operations. It determines when, where, and how production of a job will occur.

Production Credit Association A government-sponsored, short-term lending organization assisting the financing needs of farmers. Loans may be made for operating expenses, capital requirements of crop and livestock enterprises, living expenses, and family needs.

production management Management of manufacturing operations, which include inventory control, production control, purchasing, materials handling, quality control, and other functions.

production workers Production workers are skilled or semiskilled persons engaged in the processing, fabricating, assembling, receiving, inspecting, and handling of the raw material and of semi-finished and finished products, as well as those concerned with warehousing, packing, shipping, and maintenance.

product item An item in a product line distinguished by price, size, or other qualities. It is often called a stockkeeping unit.

productivity Efficiency of production measured in terms of the amount of output in relation to input of resources carried out over a period of time.

product liability insurance Insurance providing coverage against claims or financial losses arising out of the use, handling, and consumption of a product.

product line A set of items which are closely related and marketed through similar outlets and fall within a given price range.

product market erosion A decrease in demand for a product or service, caused by the introduction of a similar product which consumers purchase as a substitute.

product mix The group of products and services offered by a particular firm.

product orientation A marketing orientation which places a great deal of emphasis on the quality of the product, its durability, and other innovations while minimizing the interaction with customers.

profit sharing A distribution of the profits of a business firm, usually at the end of the year among employees, in the form of money or shares of stock. The amounts distributed may be in accordance with a predetermined formula related to years of service of the employee, or they may be allocated by a designated committee or manager without regard to previous service.

profit-sharing plan A formal plan under which employees share in the company's profits, usually in relation to their salary and service. Profits may be distributed at the end of each year or deferred until the person retires, leaves, or otherwise directs that payment be made.

pro forma According to a prescribed form or model.

pro forma statement A financial or an accounting statement projecting income and performance of business activity within a period of time, usually one to five years, based upon estimates, assumptions, and anticipated changes.

program budget A budget in which expenditures are based primarily on programs of work and secondarily on character and object. A program budget is a transitional type of budget between the traditional character-and-object budget, on the one hand, and the performance budget, on the other. *See* zero-based budgeting.

program evaluation and review technique (PERT) This is a management-control tool and a project-planning technique similar to the critical path method, which additionally includes obtaining a pessimistic, a most likely, and an optimistic time for each activity from which is computed the most likely completion time for the project along the critical path. *See* critical path method.

progressive tax A tax whose percentage rate increases as the tax base increases. Usually, such a tax has a maximum, which limits the exposure to top-bracket taxpayers.

progress payments Payments made by a lender at stages of a construction or manufacturing program as it moves toward completion.

project financing An investment banking approach that builds a viable financing arrangement (which could include equity and/or debt financing) for a given project by taking into account tax benefits, cash flows, expected rates of return, warranties and insurance, money market conditions, contractual covenants, and other factors.

project notes Issued by municipalities to finance federally sponsored urban renewal and housing programs. They are guaranteed by the U.S. Department of Housing and Urban Development, and are exempt from federal income taxation.

promotion A position change that increases one's responsibility and pay. Also, enhanced marketing activities which may be channeled through various media forms, including trade or consumer discounts, free trial periods, and raffles.

property damage liability insurance Insurance against financial losses resulting from a policyholder's liability for damage to the property of another, including loss of the use of the property.

property insurance Insurance offering financial protection against the loss of or damage to real and personal property as a result of specified perils.

property tax A tax levied by state and local governments on real estate, jewelry, and other personal holdings. Property tax is usually levied after an annual assessment of property in a community. The tax is considered a proportional tax.

property tax abatement A reduction in the amount of tax imposed upon a property, usually for no more than twenty years.

proportional tax A tax whose percentage rate remains constant as the tax base increases, so that the amount of tax paid is a fixed proportion of the tax base. Property tax is an example.

proprietary lease A lease issued by a cooperative residence association. Such leases grant the association the right to occupy the residence under certain circumstances, such as nonpayment of maintenance charges.

prorate An assignment of a portion of a cost to an operation, activity, or product according to some method or formula.

prospectus A detailed statement issued by a company or governmental entity prior to its sale of securities. The prospectus lists all the facts and information about the issuer and the offering as required for private corporations by the Securities and Exchange Commission and other regulatory bodies. In its prospectus, an issuer is required to disclose the risks and realistic prospects of the business or project it intends to conduct or service. A prospectus is required for the public underwriting and distribution of securities. For private placements, a much shorter placement memorandum is utilized. *See* going public; red herring.

proxy A legal authorization given to a person to act for another, as in a meeting of stockholders of a corporation.

prudent man rule Applied as an investment standard in some states, the legal requirement that a fiduciary, such as a trustee, may invest the fund's money only in specific securities, usually low-risk and safe instruments.

public authority A governmental unit or public agency created to perform a single function or a restricted group of related activities. Usually, such units are financed from service charges, fees, and tolls, but in some instances they also have taxing powers. An authority may be completely independent of other governmental units, or in some cases it may be partially dependent upon other units or agencies for its creation, its financing, or the exercise of certain powers.

public body Any group that has an interest in an organization's ability to achieve its objectives.

publicity Media exposure in a market which may be the result of the work of a public relations firm, or generated from the timely (i.e., in the news) nature of the activity.

public liability insurance A general term applied to forms of both bodily injury and property damage liability. It protects the insured against claims brought by members of the public.

public offering An offering by an investment banking syndicate of an original issue of stocks and bonds through public sale. Municipalities and governmental entities also have public offerings. *See* private placement.

public relations Any form of communication, including publicity, intended to promote goodwill or to create in the public mind a favorable image of the business, organization, or product. *See* advertising.

public service advertising A message which usually champions a cause or supports an issue while promoting the goodwill of the entity sponsoring the advertisement.

public utility A company providing electricity, gas, telephone, water, transportation, or other services to a large group of people. The rates these companies charge are usually regulated by state public service commissions.

pull strategy A saturation-advertising campaign intended to create consumer demand for the product.

pumped storage An arrangement whereby additional electric power may be generated during peak-load periods by hydraulic means, using water pumped into a storage reservoir during off-peak periods.

purchase agent A person responsible for buying raw materials, supplies, or equipment. Also known as a buyer or middleman who is responsible for selecting among alternative products and services available in the market.

purchase option In leasing, an option to purchase leased property at the end of the lease term.

In other forms of business, a contractual covenant that allows the renter to buy the property at a specified price and for a set period of time.

purchase order An administrative document used when buying goods or materials, indicating the quantities and specifications desired. Also, a purchaser's document used to formalize a purchase transaction with a vendor.

push strategy A marketing technique which calls for using the sales force and trade promotion to push the product through the channels of distribution.

put A contract to have the option to sell a security at a price within a stated time. A put is the opposite of a call. *See* call.

Q

quality control An engineering technique of monitoring the manufacturing process for product quality within established tolerance limits. Statistical sampling is used to verify that the desired levels of quality are reached as a result of such monitoring. *See* acceptance sampling.

quantity discount A discount in dollars or in percent, allowed on the basis that the buyer will purchase a given quantity of merchandise.

queue A waiting line. In manufacturing, the jobs at a certain work center waiting to be processed. As queues increase, so do average queue time and work-in-process inventory.

quick ratio *See* acid test ratio.

R

random access A computer storage device in which access to a particular address is such that the time required to transfer a unit of information to or from storage is independent of the location or address which is accessed. *See* multiple access.

random dispatching rule In manufacturing, the sequencing of job elements to be run on a basis that is unrelated to any measure of effectiveness for that operation.

random sampling In statistical analysis, a selection of observations taken entirely by chance and in such a way that every individual or unit of measurement has an equal and independent probability of being included in the sample.

random walk A stock market theory which states that future stock market prices and corporate earnings do not follow any predictable patterns.

ratchet demand clause A clause in an electric rate schedule which provides that maximum past or present demands be taken into account in order to establish billings for previous or subsequent periods.

rate base The value established by a regulatory authority upon which a utility is permitted to earn a specified rate of return.

rate fixing The power of a state or municipal regulatory body to set the rates a company, often a public utility, may charge its customers.

rate of exchange The daily rate at which the currency of one country can be exchanged for the currency of another country.

rate of return The income per investment period divided by the asset value at the beginning of the investment period.

rate of sale A retail activity measured by adding the opening inventory, then adding the purchases received during the period and subtracting the inventory on hand.

ratings A measurement of investment quality, obtained by the rating agencies (usually Moody's or Standard and Poor's or by institutional investors) after a review of the financial history, management, and other factors connected with a financing.

raw material Any product which is used as a component in the manufacturing process of finished products.

Reaganomics A government policy established in the administration of President Ronald Reagan which holds that a large reduction in government expenditures and simultaneous across-the-board tax cuts will encourage economic growth and reduce the level of inflation in the economy. *See* supply-side economics.

real estate investment trust An investment fund established with monies pooled from persons or entities who have joined together to invest in specific real estate projects.

real estate syndicate A joint-venture arrangement formed for buying and selling real estate projects and for sheltering income, usually during the early years of a project.

realize To convert into cash or other receivables through the sale or exchange of goods or services.

real property Classified as land, buildings, trees, minerals, and related rights or interests.

real-time program A type of computer program that continuously reacts to new input data.

reappropriation A congressional action to restore the obligational availability, whether for the same or different purposes, of all or part of the unobligated portion of the budget authority in an expired account.

receipt of goods In shipping, a stipulation that discounts and invoice dates start with the receipt of the merchandise.

receivable Any collectible item, whether or not it is currently due.

receiver A person appointed by a court to protect the interests of lenders and creditors. *See* bankrupt.

recession A moderate downturn of business activity evidenced by increased unemployment and reduced consumption. Depression is a severe form of recession.

recision The cancellation or annulment of a transaction or contract by the exercise of legal covenant or by mutual consent.

reconciliation accounting A summary of the details of the difference between any two or more accounts.

reconciliation process, congressional A process used by the U.S. Congress to reconcile amounts determined by tax, spending, and debt legislation for a given fiscal year, with the ceilings enacted in the second required concurrent resolution on the budget for that year. *See* concurrent resolution of the budget.

reconsignment A shipping arrangement whereby goods may be forwarded to a location other than the original destination without being removed from the transportation vehicle, and at the through rate from the initial point to that of final delivery.

recourse debt financing A transaction in which the lender holds the borrower liable for the financial obligations incurred. This is a requirement if the underlying collateral—equipment, land, building, or securities—is not sufficient for the loan. *See* nonrecourse debt financing.

redemption The retirement of stocks or bonds by the issuer by means of repurchase, usually at a preagreed rate, sometimes with penalties.

redemption period The time allowed by the foreclosure laws of some states during which a mortgagor may buy back property by paying the amount owed on a foreclosed mortgage, including the interest and fees. *See* equity of redemption.

red herring In corporate or municipal financings, the preliminary prospectus containing all the disclosure information required by federal, state, and local regulatory bodies and by financial industry standards, except the offering price and coupon of a new issue. *See* prospectus.

refinancing The repayment of a debt from the proceeds of a new debt issue, using the same or different collateral as security.

refunding bonds A financial transaction in which bonds or notes are issued to retire securities already outstanding. The refunding bonds may be sold for cash and outstanding bonds may be redeemed in cash, or the refunding bonds may be exchanged with holders of outstanding bonds under special requirements established in the indenture or at the time of the refinancing. *See* advance refunding bonds.

refunds Cash payment or purchase credit given to people who have repaid obligations, including taxes, fees, and assessments.

registered representative An employee of a broker-dealer who has met the requirements of the New York Stock Exchange as to background and knowledge of the securities business.

registered trademark A trademark filed with the U.S. Patent Office, giving the owner an exclusive use of the trademark.

regression analysis A statistical method for predicting a variable from a set of correlated data.

regressive tax A tax which takes a larger percentage of the income of poor persons than it does from those persons in higher income brackets. Generally, a flat rate tax which does not fluctuate with income.

regular way settlement Specific requirements which mandate the payment in cash for government securities, stocks, and bonds. If the account is not settled in time, the broker has the right to sell out the securities and bill the customer for any losses.

Regulation M Federal Reserve Board regulation requiring member banks to hold reserves against their net borrowings from their foreign branches.

Regulation Q Federal Reserve Board regulation which has the power to set the maximum rates member banks may pay on time and savings deposits.

Regulation T Federal Reserve Board regulation which has the power to set the maximum amount of credit that may be granted by brokers and dealers for the purpose of purchasing securities.

Regulation U Federal Reserve Board regulation which has the power to set the maximum amount of credit that may be granted by a bank to customers for the purpose of purchasing securities.

rehabilitation The restoration of property to a satisfactory condition without changing the style of a structure. For certain structures, federal, state, and local tax benefits or incentives may apply.

reimbursement Repayment of monies or other assets advanced in a transaction.

reinsurance The assumption by one insurance company of all or part of a risk undertaken by another insurance company.

release clause A stipulation in a contract, mortgage, or deed of trust that a portion of the security be released from the lien if certain conditions are met, such as the payment of specific sums.

remainderman A person who has received an interest in an estate.

remote job entry The use of a computer terminal to cause a job to be run on a computer.

renewal option An option to renew the lease or contract at the end of the initial term. A fee may have to be paid for such an option.

rent-up period The time after construction that a rental property requires to achieve projected stabilized income and occupancy levels.

reopen an issue A debt management policy of the U.S. Treasury of selling new securities of an existing issue rather than creating a new series or coupon issue.

reorder period The length of time between the inventory counts before periodic reordering takes place.

replacement cost The cost of replacing property without a deduction for depreciation.

replacement cost accounting An accounting technique of valuing assets at their current replacement cost.

reproduction cost The cost to reproduce, at prevailing prices, an item of property currently owned.

repurchase agreement An agreement by a firm to buy back, under certain terms, the securities which it originally sold to the second party of the transaction. *See* open repurchase agreement.

requisition A request to the purchasing department, or to another department, for specified articles or services which are needed to carry out the normal business activities of the firm.

reserve An account which establishes a portion of the fund balance and is pledged for some future use, and which is not available for further appropriation or expenditure.

reserve accounts for balance of payments The accounts reflecting the changes in the amount of resources that the government of a country has available to settle international payments.

Reserve requirements The deposits of member banks of the Federal Reserve Banks, held under regulation of the Federal Reserve Board.

residual value The value of equipment at the conclusion of the lease term.

responsibility The obligation of a subordinate to perform tasks assigned to him by superiors.

restraint of trade Business combinations or contracts by business firms that tend to lessen or eliminate competition. This process also increases prices and limits the choice of goods available in the marketplace.

restrictive covenant A clause in a contract limiting the use of the property for a certain period of time and for certain purposes.

retail advertising Advertising of a local nature by area merchants who sell directly to the consumer.

retailing A business activity mainly concerned with selling to final consumers.

retainage (retention) The amount, usually 10 to 20 percent, which is withheld from payment to contractors or subcontractors as per contractual agreement, in order to insure a final and satisfactory completion of the job. Also known as retention.

retained earnings Accumulated net income, less distributions to stockholders and transfers to paid-in capital accounts.

retirement A voluntary or forced severance of employment because of age, disability, or illness. Generally, the individual withdraws permanently from gainful work and lives on a retirement allowance or pension.

return on equity The net income after debt service, expressed as a percentage of the owners' equity.

return on investment (ROI) The net project income divided by the average investment in the project during a given period.

revenue The monetary value of a product, merchandise, rent, dividend, or service rendered.

revenue anticipation notes The obligations issued by states, municipalities, or public authorities to finance current expenditures in anticipation of the future receipt of revenues, governmental aid, or other fees.

revenue bonds Bonds whose principal and interest are payable exclusively from earnings on a public enterprise. In addition to a pledge of revenues, such bonds sometimes contain a mortgage on the enterprise's property.

revenue ruling A written opinion of the Internal Revenue Service requested by concerned parties. It is applicable only to those facts described in the request for the opinion. A private-letter ruling, if issued, in contrast to a normal public ruling, may not be relied on for a general interpretation of the applicable regulations.

revenue tariff A tariff on imports, levied for the purpose of producing tax revenue.

reverse annuity mortgage (RAM) Provides a stream of monthly payments to homeowners through an annuity purchased by a loan against their accumulated equity in the house.

reverse repurchase agreements These transactions are entered into by dealers to cover short positions in securities. If the Federal Reserve System is engaging in reverse repurchase agreements, it is borrowing money from the financial markets.

revocable letter of credit An instrument which may be revoked at any time by the company or by the issuing bank. It may be used when a high degree of trust exists between buyer and seller, between affiliated companies, or when the underlying commodity is readily salable at a nondepreciated price in the open market. *See* irrevocable letter of credit.

right of way A temporary or permanent easement permitting the construction and operation of a railway, road, power line, or pipeline over land belonging to another party.

right to work laws Laws passed by individual states to permit workers the right to work without having to join a union.

risk Any course of action which has a degree of uncertainty or where loss is possible. Through strategic planning, insurance, and other methods, the risk element could be minimized.

risk analysis An analytic technique which weighs situations by introducing probabilities in order to give a more accurate assessment of the risks involved.

risk manager An insurance specialist who may be employed by the firm or serves as an independent consultant, and who evaluates risks to which a project or enterprise may be subjected. He then prescribes appropriate action with respect to insurance coverage, including self-insurance.

risk premium A payment required to compensate for a particular risk. The greater the risk, the larger the premium.

robotics An industrial and commercial application of automated devices in performing certain specialized tasks. As the control, memory, and dexterity of the machines improve, the use of the devices in automation is greatly enhanced.

role A set of activities that an individual is supposed to perform according to the formal requirements and expectations of the individual and the persons in authority over him.

roll-over mortgage (ROM) A renegotiated loan for which the interest rate and monthly payments are renegotiated (typically) every five years. The rate is usually adjusted according to current market conditions.

roll over The reinvestment of maturing securities into similar or different maturing instruments.

routing Assigning a sequence to the various steps in a manufacturing or other process.

royalty Compensation for the use of property, usually copyrighted material or natural resources, expressed as a percentage of the income derived from using the property or service.

runaway shop A manufacturing establishment which moves from one location to another primarily to escape the unionization of its employees or the application of labor laws.

running the books In the underwriting of securities, the senior managing underwriter, in nearly all cases, has the responsibility for keeping control over the orders received by and the marketing activities of the syndicate. The underwriter is in charge of allocating securities to other underwriters, members of the sales group, and certain large investors. *See* senior managing underwriter.

S

safe harbor guidelines Under the Economic Recovery Tax Act of 1981, requirements imposed by law on leasing transactions in order to determine the parameters of a true lease for tax purposes.

salary Payments made to employees on a weekly, biweekly, or monthly basis.

sale An agreement between two parties concerning the transfer of property under certain conditions, including the amount of funds to be paid, the date on which the property is to be transferred, the condition of the property at the time of transfer, and a second mortgage, if any, taken back by the owner.

sale-leaseback A transaction involving the sale of the property by the owner and a lease of the property back to the seller, usually on a long-term basis. The seller benefits from the cash payment, and the buyer benefits from a good return on his investment and the use of the tax benefits of the facility.

sales against cash deposit in advance A seller or exporter, under certain credit risk conditions, may require a cash deposit in advance to shipping the material to the buyer.

sales allowance A reduction in price that is usually given because the goods received by the buyer are not exactly what was ordered or were not received at the time expected.

sales budget An estimate of the expected volume of sales. It is used primarily for making current purchasing, production, and cash-flow decisions. The budget is formalized after a careful review of market conditions, general economic trends, and other factors.

sales discount A sales price reduction or allowance usually offered for prompt or early payments.

sales forecast An estimate of the expected sales, by product class, service, and price, and by territory for a period of time in the future.

sales on a consignment basis In foreign trade, an arrangement in which the selling agent holds merchandise against regular payment.

sales promotion Marketing activities designed to increase consumption and demand, sometimes called demand creation or demand stimulation. Promotion includes premium plans, trade shows, sampling, sales meetings, sweepstakes, sales films, and joint sales techniques.

sales-response function The likely sales level for a specific category of marketing effort.

sales tax A tax based upon a percentage of the receipts of a sale. Usually levied by state and local governments.

salvage value The realized selling price, less the cost of disposition of an asset in the form of second-hand material, junk, or scrap. (For insurance purposes, the value of the item after a fire, wreck, or disaster.)

sampling A statistical procedure for obtaining a valid estimate where it is either impossible or too costly to make a total count or census.

saturation marketing A market condition for a product where new sales are originated by replacing the old product with the new one of the same kind.

savings and loan associations Federal or state-chartered thrift institutions that offer savings deposit services to individuals and invest the bulk of their funds into residential mortgages.

seasonal variations Regular, recurring fluctuations confined to a specific time period.

seasoned issue In the underwriting process of new issues of securities, an issue that has been well distributed, and trades according to expectations in the secondary market.

secondary data Data that already exist in reference form, since they have been collected from primary sources. *See* primary data.

secondary financing Usually a financing involving a second mortgage which is junior to the first mortgage. The interest rate on a second mortgage may be higher or lower than the rate on the first.

secondary market A trading market in which outstanding securities of corporations, government agencies, and municipalities are sold and purchased through dealers registered to conduct such business.

secondary mortgage market A national market in which existing mortgages are bought and sold. Mortgages are sold on a package basis and must have good documentations. Contrasts with the primary market where mortgages are originated.

secondary offering The selling of a large block of securities currently held by large stockholders, such as officers of the corporation. The Securities and Exchange Commission has specific requirements for these offerings, including the holding period for the stocks before the sale, the amount of the offering, and the frequency of the distribution. Also referred to as secondary distribution.

second mortgage A real estate mortgage which is junior to another mortgage in terms of the mortgagee's or subordinate's claim on some asset. *See* junior mortgage.

secured credit A loan or credit line backed by collateral. It is required when the credit risk associated with the borrower requires additional pledged assets, such as securities or property.

secured party A lender who has a lien on a property or asset or is the beneficiary of certain pledges or guarantees.

Securities and Exchange Commission A United States regulatory agency responsible for protecting the investing public. It registers all corporate securities, monitors fraud and the business activities of brokers, and investigates any irregular practices of market participants.

security A property, asset, or pledge given by a borrower to a lender to satisfy the credit conditions established by the lender's departments for credit and investment.

security agreement An agreement between a secured party and a debtor creating a security interest in an asset or property.

security deposit Money (usually one month's rent) deposited by a tenant with a landlord as security for the full and faithful performance by the tenant of the terms of the lease.

security instrument In mortgage finance, the mortgage or trust deed that evidences the pledge of real estate security as distinguished from another credit instrument.

security interest Under the Uniform Commercial Codes, a term designating the interest of the creditor in the property of the debtor in all types of credit transactions. *See* collateral.

selective distortion The tendency of people to twist information into meanings other than those meant by impartial parties.

selective distribution A method of distributing a product or service which is profitable, easy to manage or control, and is not inconsistent with other marketing, production, or financial efforts.

self-insurance An arrangement established by some firms, governmental agencies, and individuals to assume all or a portion of their own losses. Self-insurers often establish special funds for this purpose. Insurance is purchased to cover losses in excess of predetermined levels.

seller's market A market condition in which goods or services are scarce, therefore, buyers compete among themselves to obtain supplies or services. *See* buyer's market.

selling concept A marketing approach which assumes that consumers will not buy enough of a company's product unless a major effort is made to stimulate their interest in the product.

selling group When a new issue of securities is large, the managing underwriter of the syndicate may form a group of broker/dealers, who are given the opportunity to sell the securities on a fixed commission at the offering price.

semiconductor A type of memory unit composed of a number of integrated-circuit chips mounted on a printed circuit board.

senior debt Debt which has the first claim against a company's earnings and assets. *See* first mortgage.

seniority The length of service as defined in the labor contract of an employee in his total employment or in some particular unit of the plant in which he works. There are no enforceable seniority rights without a collective bargaining agreement.

senior managing underwriter An investment or a commercial banking firm responsible for managing a syndicate of underwriters in negotiating or bidding for bond or stock issues of corporations, public authorities, and other governments. The contractual relationship between the senior managing underwriter and the members of the syndicate is governed by an agreement among underwriters. *See* running the books.

separation Voluntary or involuntary severance from a job.

serial bond A bond issue in which the principal is repaid in periodic installments over the life of the financing. *See* term bond.

series discount An offering of more than one trade discount by a manufacturer to a purchaser.

service Work performed by individuals or firms that is essentially intangible. Information, legal services, entertainment, and security are examples.

service departments An organizational grouping comprised of functional specialists responsible for assisting other departments or units of the firm.

service mark A word or name used in the sale or advertising of services to identify those of one person or firm and to distinguish them from those of others.

servomechanism A feedback control system in which at least one of the system signals represents mechanical motion.

settlement date A date established by rules or conventions on which a particular security is delivered against funds. The date may be the trade date or a later date.

share An evidence of equity ownership in a corporation, in which ownership interest is related to the number of shares owned.

shipping release A form used by the purchaser to specify shipping instructions of goods purchased for delivery at some future date or destination.

shopping a bid The process of searching for the best bid (or offer) available by calling a number of intermediaries.

short covering Buying stock to return stock previously borrowed to make delivery on a short sale.

short selling In stock trading, the procedure of selling stock one does not own by borrowing it from one's broker. The short seller hopes to replace the stock by buying it later at a lower price and thus profit from the difference between the price at which he sold it and that for which he purchased it back at the later time.

short-term Ordinarily, relates to a period less than one year.

short-term debt Debt with a maturity of one year or less. In municipal finance, "short"-term notes have been issued for up to three years in maturity. *See* long-term debt.

sick benefits A payment made to a sick worker through participation in private or union-managed insurance programs and in state-established disability programs. *See* fringe benefits.

sight draft An order usually payable upon presentation or delivery, sometimes with supporting documentation. *See* time draft.

silent partner A member of a partnership whose interests are generally financing and who does not take an active part in the organization.

simple interest The interest earned from the principal amount only. *See* compound interest.

simulation The representation of certain features of the characteristics of a physical or abstract system by the behavior of another system. Computer programs can simulate complex systems and find optimal solutions to given problems.

single-discount equivalent Represents the equivalent of the series discount offered by a company and is expressed as a single percentage.

sinking fund Assets and their earnings earmarked in a segregated fund for the retirement of bonds.

Small Business Administration A unit of the U.S. Department of Commerce which provides financial, procurement, and management assistance to small business concerns, and also assists victims of natural and other disasters. The financial aid offered to small business firms includes both direct loans and guaranteed loans.

small claims court Courts set up for the express purpose of settling minor claims between parties. Decisions in such litigations are made by a judge within a short period of time, thereby avoiding a prolonged court case.

social classes Groups of people who share interests, religion, financial positions, academic background, and other values.

social safety net A term developed during President Reagan's administration describing the minimum combination of government programs necessary to sustain the truly needy segment of the population.

Social Security Act A federal law mandating unemployment benefits, health insurance, disability benefits, and other aid to needy or elderly persons and families.

societal marketing concept A marketing orientation which develops products and services in harmony with consumer needs and in concert with broader societal standards and needs.

soft loan A loan, usually made by the World Bank or other development banks, bearing either no interest rate or a rate that is below the true cost of the capital loaned. The lending bank may also take a currency risk in which the loan is repaid in borrower's currency rather than in dollars or equivalent hard currencies.

software The programs, documents, routines, and compilers used in or with computers; all computer-related materials that are not hardware items.

space discount Given by a publication for the volume of advertising a company uses.

span of control A management practice which holds that a supervisor, manager, or executive cannot operate efficiently if he has more than a limited number of junior managers reporting directly to him. Generally, the higher the level of work, the smaller the number of persons directly reporting to the senior manager. This concept excludes staff aides and assistants who act on behalf of the executives in carrying out specific functions. *See* management.

special drawing rights Money created by the International Monetary Fund with the approval of the majority of the member countries and distributed among all member countries. This paper money is used only in transactions among governments and between governments and the Fund.

specialization To carry out complex tasks or to increase the volume production, organizations divide the production and distribution process into functions and market areas. This concept usually enhances efficiency and increases the profitability of the enterprise.

specialty goods A product with unique attributes and a defined brand image which a significant number of buyers are habitually willing to purchase.

specialty store A store which offers an extensive selection of goods within a limited variety of merchandise.

specific duties A levy on imports made as a fixed charge per physical unit, volume, length, or weight.

speculative transaction A transaction in which the eventual net return or cost is not known in advance or in which the probability of success is very modest.

spending authority In the congressional budgetary process, a collective designation for borrowing authority, contract authority, and entitlement authority, for which the budget authority is not provided in advance by appropriation acts.

spinoff The transfer by a corporation of a portion of its assets, which may include a subsidiary to a newly formed company in exchange for the latter's capital stock. *See* subsidiary corporation.

split run The placing of different advertisements in alternate copies of the same issue of a newspaper or magazine.

sponsor The company or individual paying for talent and broadcasting time in a radio or television program.

spot market The market for buying and selling commodities.

spot rate Foreign exchange rate for currency delivered within a specified number of days.

spread The difference between two prices, such as between a bid and an asked price or between the price paid and that received for a product. In underwriting stocks or bonds, the spread is the difference between what the investment banker sells the securities for and the amount of funds the issuer receives.

square position Position when the cash inflows match the cash outflows in a given currency for a certain date or period of time.

staff An organizational position where the person serves in an advisory capacity to others, particularly to individuals in line positions. *See* line.

stagflation A business condition characterized by the simultaneous occurrence of rising prices and insufficient economic expansion. This combination usually causes an increase in unemployment and a rise in interest rates. *See* inflation.

standard deviation A measure of the dispersion of data points available around their mean value.

standard industrial classification The division of all industry, into detailed standard classifications, identified by code numbers.

standardization Using uniform methods and procedures in manufacturing.

Standard Metropolitan Statistical Area A designation of population centers, defined by the U.S. Office of Management and Budget on a county-line basis.

standby commitment A contract or agreement made for a limited period as security for a construction lender by an investor who stands ready to make or purchase the committed loan at agreed-on terms.

standby fee The fee charged by an investor for a standby commitment, which is paid at the time the commitment is entered into.

standby letter of credit An instrument drawn by a bank securing a transaction or the performance of certain parties. The time duration, the monetary coverage, and the fee charged for the service are established by the financial institution.

standby space An extra discount given to an advertiser if he gives an option to a newspaper as to the time his advertisement will run in the publication.

stated capital The capital of a corporation contributed by stockholders.

statements Presentations of financial data which show the financial position and the results of financial operations of a fund, a group of accounts, or an entire governmental unit for a particular accounting period.

statistical demand analysis A set of statistical procedures designed to discover the most important real factors affecting sales and their relative influence on consumer buying patterns.

statistical error An inaccuracy arising in measurements of the average count rate for random events as a result of statistical fluctuations in the rate.

statistical universe A population of things or data which have common characteristics for the stated purpose of the statistical analysis.

step-down lease A lease whose terms and conditions call for one initial rent followed by decreases in rent over stated periods of time.

step-up lease A lease whose terms and conditions call for one initial rent followed by increases in rent over stated periods of time.

stochastic A problem-solving method of direct solution by trial and error, usually without a step-by-step approach, and involving analysis and an evaluation of the progress made, as in a heuristic approach to trial-and-error methods.

stock option The right given by a corporation to purchase a specified number of shares of stock for a specified price and at specified times.

stock power A power of attorney permitting a person other than the owner of the stock to transfer legally the title of ownership to a third party. Stock powers are usually given when stock is pledged as collateral to loans.

stock shortages The shrinkage of merchandise inventory through loss or theft.

stock turnover An index of the speed with which the merchandise moves in and out of the store or department.

stop-payment order A depositor's instruction to his bank to refuse payment of a specified check he has issued. A bank usually charges a penalty for such an order.

storage A device or a piece of equipment which receives data, holds it, and at a later time returns the data.

straddle An option strategy involving the purchase of one put and one call or the sale of one put and one call. *See* strip, strap.

straight-line depreciation Depreciation taken evenly in a fixed percentage over the depreciable life of a capital asset.

strap An option combination consisting of two call options and one put, all with the same strike price and expiration date. *See* strip, straddle.

strategic planning A process of developing and maintaining a strategic fit between the organization and its changing business opportunities. Clear company mission, objectives and goals, growth strategies, and product portfolios have to be developed if an optimal plan is to be established.

strike A temporary stoppage of work by workers who have a grievance or who demand better wages and job conditions. *See* dispute.

strip An option combination of two put options and one call, all with the same strike price and expiration date. *See* strap, straddle.

subcontracting An arrangement made by a general contractor to have part or all of his product serviced or manufactured by another, independent contractor.

sublease A lease given by a lessee to a third party for a term not longer than the remaining portion of the original lease.

subordinated agreement A claim that is junior vis-à-vis other claims against an asset or property.

subordinated debenture The claims of holders of this security rank after those of holders of various other debts incurred by the corporation.

subordination clause A covenant in a junior mortgage enabling the first lien to keep its priority in case of renewal or refinancing.

subrogation The legal process by which an insurance company, after paying a loss, seeks to recover the amount of the loss from the party legally responsible for the loss.

subroutine A computer program that defines desired operations and which may be included in another program to produce the desired operations.

subsidiary corporation A business enterprise which is controlled by another company through ownership of a majority of the outstanding shares. *See* spinoff.

subsidy A financial incentive given by a government or agency for the purpose of carrying out the stated objectives of a grant award. A subsidy may assist an operation of a program, the capital financing of a facility, or it may encourage the consumption of a product or service.

sum-of-the-years' digits An accelerated depreciation technique in which the estimated life of an asset is used to compute progressively smaller depreciation amounts.

sunk cost This cost usually will not impact the future decision-making process concerning a particular project.

supplemental appropriation A congressional act appropriating funds in addition to those in an annual appropriation act. Supplemental appropriations provide additional budget authority beyond the original estimates for programs or activities.

suppliers Business firms, such as wholesalers, who supply resources needed by the producer manufacturing the particular good or service.

supply The ability and willingness of producers to sell their goods and services for a particular price at a specific time. The higher the price, the more willing the producers are to sell their products; demand, however, may drop for some goods as prices rise. *See* demand.

supply-side economics A business and economic philosophy which states that economic growth and consumer demand are limited by the level of production that needs to be stimulated in contrast to consumption, which, in the aggregate, is unlimited. To encourage production and reduce inflation, maximum tax incentives, deregulation, and governmental budgetary cutbacks must be put in place. *See* Reaganomics.

surety A person or company who guarantees the performance of another. Also known as suretyship. *See* performance bond; performance standards.

surety bond A contract providing for financial compensation should there be a failure to perform specific steps within a stated period of time.

swap currency position A trade when a given currency is simultaneously purchased and sold, but the maturity of each of the transactions is different.

swap currency rate Forward exchange rates, expressed in terms of premiums or discounts from the spot rate.

sweepstakes A promotion campaign in which prizewinners are determined on the basis of a random drawing alone. No purchase is necessary.

sweetener Any incentive provided to a purchaser which positively impacts his decision making. In bond underwriting, a sweetener could be a warrant given by the issuer to the investors, which could be exercised at a given interest rate. The objective of the issuer is to obtain a lower interest cost for his financing. *See* warrant.

syndicate An association of persons or firms who join together to share the risks and profits as well as the legal liabilities of a project. Syndicates are formed in such areas as insurance underwriting, investment banking, and real estate. Horses, stamps, and diamonds have been purchased by syndicates.

system An organization of computer hardware, software, and/or people, assembled to complete a set of tasks with defined objectives and purposes.

system assembly A programming software system which includes a programming language and a group of machine-language programs.

system backup Error detection and correction techniques that diagnose and correct computer and transmission errors.

systems analysis A method of solving problems and making decisions by applying statistical methods and computer technology. One of the prime objectives of a systems analysis is to define the boundaries of the problems being studied. The work is conducted in business, industrial, and governmental sectors.

system support A collection of computer programs used to aid the production and check-out of a system.

T

T account An accounting format shaped like the letter T. Debits are shown to the left and credits to the right of the vertical line.

tacit understanding An informal understanding, i.e., a gentleman's agreement, which may be implied but is not committed to writing or a formal contract.

tactics The development of arrangements and procedures for a process or activity, with alternate priorities for accomplishing the goals and objectives set forth. *See* fallback options.

Taft-Hartley Act A federal law which lists unfair labor practices. It also specifies the rights of employees and employers in labor relations, including the circumstances under which a strike may not be legally called.

take and pay contract A legally binding agreement which stipulates payment by a party only in an event that the products or services have been delivered according to preagreed specifications.

takedown In mortgage finance, the drawing of needed funds against a previously made loan commitment. In the underwriting of securities, the expected compensation, i.e., commission, a syndicate member will receive by taking down a block of bonds.

take or pay contract An agreement which commits a party to purchase specific goods at a predetermined price. If the goods are not bought, the party providing the purchase commitment must pay an amount equal to the cost of the goods it had committed to buy.

takeout commitment A commitment received by a builder and required by a construction lender which specifies that long-term mortgage funds will be available to pay off the construction lender after the building has been completed.

takeout loan A first mortgage loan which is committed and expected to be made upon the completion of a specific real estate construction project, paying off the construction lenders.

talking computer A specially designed instructional computer for a blind person, who types in information on a keyboard and receives responses from a voice synthesizer.

target market A well-defined set of customers whose needs the company plans to satisfy.

target marketing Selecting one or more of the market segments and developing a specific strategy for each.

tariff A government-imposed tax or duty placed on imported goods.

tariff systems Provide either a single rate of duty for each item, applicable to all countries, or two or more rates, applicable to different countries or groups of countries.

tax A revenue source of federal and state and local governments. The yield from any tax depends on economic conditions and the enforcement procedures followed by the tax collectors.

tax adjustment clause A clause in a rate schedule that provides for an adjustment in the customer's bill if the supplier experiences a change in the tax rate from a specified base or from the application of new taxes.

tax anticipation notes Issued by states or municipalities to finance current needs in anticipation of future tax receipts. The total of these notes, which may be issued by a governmental body, is limited by state constitutions or by other legal methods.

tax expenditures Losses of tax revenues attributable to provisions of the federal tax laws, which allow a special exclusion, exemption, or deduction from gross income, or which provide a special credit, a preferential rate of tax, or a deferral of tax liability.

tax haven A country that imposes little or no tax on the profits from the transactions carried on from that country.

tax rate The amount of tax stated in terms of a unit of the tax base.

tax shelter A general term used to describe a wide variety of transactions which defer the payment of taxes by reducing the effective taxable income of a person or corporation. In most cases, the level of tax reduction or deferral is related to the direct financial liability at risk in an arrangement.

technological forecasting Forecasting the future and its impact on the operations of an enterprise.

telecommunications Data transmission between communications systems and remotely located devices via a unit that performs the necessary format conversion and controls the rate and sequence of transmission.

teleconferencing The use of computer systems as a communication tool among widely dispersed groups of people.

teleprinter A printing device that combines a keyboard and a printer.

teleprocessing The processing of information received from or sent to remote locations over communications lines.

telex A direct teletype transmission between two points, usually on a dial-up basis. Charges are computed for the time of transmission rather than based on the number of words.

temporary import surcharges Imposed to provide extra protection to local industry, assist balance-of-payments problems, or punish certain countries which are not acting in the best interests of the United States.

tenancy at will An estate which may be terminated by either the lessor or the lessee after giving notice to the respective parties.

tenancy by entirety The joint ownership of property by a husband and wife, in which both are viewed as one person and upon the death of one, the other gets the estate.

tenancy in common A form of estate held by two or more persons, each of whom is considered as possessing the entire estate. In this case, there is no right of survivorship.

tender offer An invited public offer to buy shares from the existing stockholders of one public corporation by another company or other organization under specified terms good for a certain time period. Stockholders are asked to "tender" (surrender) their holdings for a stated value, usually at a premium above the current market price, subject to the tendering of a minimum and maximum number of shares.

term The period of time between the commencement date and the termination date of a bond, mortgage, legal document, or other contract.

term bond A bond which has a single maturity, compared with serial bonds, which have multiple maturities. *See* serial bond.

terminal A device, usually equipped with a keyboard and a display, capable of sending and receiving information over a communication channel.

termination charge Any amount not resulting from a rate schedule application which is payable by an electric system customer when service is terminated at the customer's request.

termination option A covenant in a contract or lease which permits termination under certain provisions with or without the payment of a penalty or fine.

term loan Credit extended by commercial banks for a period not more than ten years. The interest rate may be fixed or tied to some index, such as the prime lending rate.

term mortgage A mortgage loan granted for a fixed term of years, with the entire loan due at the end of that period.

terms of access for imports Conditions which apply to the importation of goods manufactured in a foreign country. Included are import duties, import restrictions or quotas, foreign exchange regulations, and preference arrangements.

text editing A computer program which permits the original keyboarding of textual copy without regard to the eventual publication format. Once the copy is in computer storage, it can be edited and justified to any required format. *See* word processing.

theory An exposition or description of an abstract principle, such as an event with a very low probability of actually happening.

theory X A management theory which assumes that the average human being has an inherent dislike of work and will avoid it if possible. It proposes that most people must be coerced, controlled, directed, threatened with punishment to get them to produce adequate effort, and that the average human being prefers to be directed, wishes to avoid responsibility, has relatively little ambition, and wants security above all.

theory Y A management theory which assumes that the expenditure of physical and mental effort in work is as natural as in play or rest. It proposes that human beings will exercise self-direction and self-control in the service of objectives to which they are committed, that commitment to objectives is a function of the rewards associated with their achievement, that the average human being accepts and seeks responsibility, and that the intellectual potentialities of the average human being are only partially utilized.

thin market A financial or commodity market in which trading volume is minimal, and in which bid and asked quotes are far apart and the liquidity of an instrument is low. *See* active market.

tie-in sale A practice whereby a seller requires the buyer to purchase one or more additional products as a condition for buying the desired product.

tie line A private communication channel linking two or more points. Such lines exist, for example, between the main and branch offices of organizations. *See* wire house.

tight market An active, liquid market with a large volume, with bid and asked prices relatively close together.

time discount Given for the frequency or regularity with which an advertiser inserts advertisements.

time draft An order usually payable within a specified time frame, generally thirty days. *See* sight draft.

time frame The general limit of time needed for a specific situation or event.

time-series analysis A business economic forecast prepared on the basis of a statistical analysis of past data.

time-sharing A method of using a computing system that allows a number of users to execute programs concurrently, and to interact with the program during execution.

times-interest earned The ratio of pretax income plus interest charges to the interest charges on long-term obligations.

title The right to ownership of real or personal property. The documentary evidence of that ownership includes a deed, certificate of title, or bill of sale.

title insurance Insurance which indemnifies the owner of real estate in the event that his or her clear ownership of property is challenged by the discovery of faults in the title. *See* certificate of title.

title search An examination of public records, laws, and court decisions to disclose the past and current facts regarding ownership of real estate. The facts disclosed may include liens, encumbrances, and easements, among other conditions.

tolerance The amount and direction (plus or minus) of the deviation from a basic dimension. Also, the allowable difference in dimensions between two interacting parts.

total energy system On-site generation of electricity, with a beneficial use of waste heat.

total market potential The maximum amount of sales for a product which might be available to all the firms in an industry during a given period, under a given level of industry marketing expenditures, and in a given economic and regulatory environment.

trade advertising Advertising directed at retailers and wholesalers.

trade association A private nonprofit organization of companies in a particular trade or industry formed for the protection and advancement of their common interests.

trade character An animated character or person created to identify the product or advertiser.

trade date The transaction date, which is usually different from the settlement date.

trade discount A discount from the list price offered to all customers of a given class, such as wholesalers and retailers.

trademark Any device, word, or symbol that identifies the origin of a product by telling who made it or who sold it.

trademark abandonment The discontinuance of the use of and right to a trademark with the intent of not resuming its use, which deprives the owner of his right to the mark.

trade name A name which applies to a business as a whole, not to an individual product.

transmission The act or process of transporting electric energy in bulk from a source or sources of supply to other principal parts of the system or to other utility systems.

transship The transfer of goods from one ship or conveyance to another; the rehandling or transshipment of items en route.

traveler's checks Represent a cashier's check of the issuing bank, and are particularly valuable as they are not negotiable when lost.

traveling display An exhibit prepared by a manufacturer of a product and loaned in rotation to various dealers.

Treasury bill A noncoupon-bearing discount security issued by the U.S. Treasury. Most bills are issued so as to mature from three months to one year.

treasury stock Capital stock issued and then reacquired by a corporation. Such reacquisitions result in a reduction of stockholders' equity.

true lease A transaction that qualifies as a lease under the Internal Revenue Code so that the lessee can claim rental payments as tax deductions, and the lessor can claim tax benefits of ownership, such as depreciation and investment credit if available for the product or facility. *See* financing lease.

trust An agreement in which property, real or personal, is held by one party for the benefit of another. It is frequently used in leases, bond issues, and financings.

trust certificate A document evidencing the beneficial ownership of a trust estate by an equity participant or other parties.

trust deed The instrument given by a borrower to a trustee, vesting title to a property in the trustee as security for the borrower's fulfillment of an obligation or contractual requirements.

trustee A bank or trust company which acts as a fiduciary and holds property or money for the benefit of another party until contractual requirements are met by the borrower. *See* fiduciary.

trustee in bankruptcy A qualified person representing the creditors who takes charge of the property to be liquidated, and is charged with the distribution of the proceeds to the creditors.

Trust Funds of the United States Funds collected and used by the federal government to carry out specific purposes and programs according to the terms of a trust agreement or statute, such as Social Security and unemployment Trust Funds. Trust Funds are administered by the government in a fiduciary capacity, and are not available for general governmental purposes. Trust-Fund receipt accounts are credited with receipts generated by the terms of the trust agreement or statute.

trust indenture A legal document that summarizes the specific conditions and terms of a trust, such as a trust to create pension funds, or a debt obligation.

Truth in Lending Laws Consumer protection laws requiring the full disclosure by sellers of the prices of items and the financing terms, interest costs, and other conditions associated with any purchase or labor. *See* consumer credit.

turbine An enclosed, rotary type of prime mover in which heat energy in steam or gas is converted into mechanical energy by the force of a high-velocity flow of steam or gases, directed against successive rows of radial blades fastened to a central shaft.

turnkey leasing The leasing to a housing authority for use by low- and moderate-income tenants of completed housing constructed by private sponsors.

turnkey project One in which a builder-contractor-developer contracts with a government or approved private agency to construct and deliver a completed facility that includes all items necessary for occupancy.

U

umbrella liability A form of insurance protection against losses in excess of the amount covered by other liability insurance policies.

underemployment A labor condition in which skilled workers hold jobs for which they are overqualified, either by education or experience. In some situations, a person may work fewer hours in order to provide other workers with employment opportunities.

underwriter A broker-dealer who agrees to purchase an entire security issue for a specified price, usually for resale to others. In some cases, he may use only his best efforts to market the securities.

underwriting Analyzing the risk elements of a financing, and attaching rates of return or premiums to compensate for the risks involved. *See* best-effort basis.

underwriting syndicate A group of firms which has joined together to distribute and sell a new offering of securities to investors. Depending on the terms of the agreement among the underwriters, the firms may individually or jointly have liability for their share of the underwriting.

unearned income Income from property, stocks, or bonds rather than from wages, salaries, or consulting fees.

unemployment insurance A state-administered program which provides income for a specific period of unemployment for persons laid off from their jobs who are willing and able to accept employment if offered. Sometimes, union pension funds supplement the unemployment paid by the state agency.

unfair labor practice An action by a union or company which interferes with the basic right of employees to join or refrain from joining labor unions and engage in collective bargaining.

unified federal budget The present form of the budget of the federal government, in which receipts and outlays from federal funds and trust funds are consolidated. When these fund groups are consolidated to display budget totals, outlays from one fund group for payment to the other fund group (i.e., interfund transactions) are deducted to avoid double counting. Transactions of off-budget federal entities are not included in the unified budget.

Uniform Commercial Code A national codification of major laws governing commerce and finance which has been adopted by almost all states. The Code covers such things as contracts, commercial paper, and bank deposits.

unilateral transfers In balance of payments, the accounts that measure gifts sent in and out of the reporting country.

uninsured motorist protection An insurance protection which covers the policyholder and his family members if injured by a hit-and-run motorist or by a driver who carries no liability insurance.

union shop An organization in which a requirement for employment is membership in a union. A worker could work in the plant or company provided he agrees to join the union at a later date. *See* modified union shop.

unit cost The cost of producing a unit of product or rendering a unit of service. These costs include labor, materials, and overhead items, which could be allocated to a product.

useful life The period of time during which the structure may reasonably be expected to perform the function for which it was designed and manufactured.

user In data processing, a person or company using a computer terminal linked to a time-sharing system and putting in data necessary for running the program.

usury Charging interest in excess of the legal rate established by law or regulation.

usury ceiling A maximum legal rate set in some states for interest, discounts, or other fees that may be charged for the use of money. The ceiling may vary depending on the nature or type of the loan, and some states have eliminated the maximum rate on certain financial transactions.

utility program A standard computer routine used in such areas as sorting or conversion.

utilization factor The ratio of the maximum demand of a system, or part of a system, to the rated capacity of the system or part of the system.

V

valuable consideration An enforceable contract based on the premise that one party agrees to do something in return for some item, money, or property the other party agrees to give him.

value analysis A cost-reduction approach whereby the relationship of design, function, and cost of any material or service is examined with the object of reducing costs. *See* methods analysis.

variable annuity A pension benefit plan that fluctuates in value with the changes in the worth of the assets, typically common stocks, in which the pension fund is invested. The variable annuity was designed to provide an adjustment mechanism for inflation, on the theory that stock prices would rise over time.

variable costing A method of cost allocation in which only the variable cost of production is applied to the product. The fixed costs of production are not attributed for cost analysis purposes.

variable costs Operating costs that vary directly with production volume; for example, materials consumed, power expenditures, direct labor, sales commissions and transportation costs.

variable export levies The object of these levies is to raise the price of imported products to the domestic level.

variable rate mortgage (VRM) The interest rate is tied to some reference index that reflects changes in market rates of interest. Thus, future monthly payments are not known at the time the loan is originated. The homeowner bears the risk of fluctuating interest rates. *See* balloon mortgage.

vendor The person who sells, or contracts to sell, the property.

venture capital Capital available for the establishment of a new business or new-product development. A venture capitalist usually requires a high return for his investment, and at times a substantial equity participation in the new business.

verbal agreement An agreement reached orally but not committed to writing; hence, it may not be a formal contract. *See* memorandum of understanding.

verification The process of checking recorded data in order to minimize human errors in data transcription or transmission.

vertical integration The expansion of a company, which could range from controlling the supply of raw materials to owning the distribution networks reaching the final customer. *See* horizontal integration.

vested interest A present or future right or privilege to partake in an endeavor or activity.

volt The unit of electromotive force or electric pressure analogous to water pressure in pounds per square inch. It is the electromotive force which, if steadily applied to a circuit having a resistance of one ohm, will produce a current of one ampere.

voluntary bankruptcy A bankruptcy initiated by the debtor rather than by the creditors.

voucher A written document which indicates the authenticity of the transactions and usually designates the accounts in which they are to be recorded.

W

wage Payments made to employees on an hourly basis. The federal and state governments have established minimum wages employers must pay employees.

wage adjustment clause A clause in a contractor's schedule that provides for an adjustment of the customer's bill if the wage scale of the employees varies from a specified standard.

Wagner Act A federal act passed in 1935, designed to promote and protect the right of employees to organize.

warehousing The care, handling, and storage of goods until they are needed to meet consumer demand.

warrant A form of security issued by a company which gives the holder the right to buy a specified number of the company's own stock shares at a specified price and within a specified period of time. Sometimes sold independently or attached to other securities as a sweetener. *See* sweetener.

warranty A contract to make up for any damages or losses that result from the failure of a product or service to perform.

watt The power of a current of one ampere flowing across a potential difference of one volt.

waybill A document prepared by a transportation company at the point of origin or shipment, giving the point of origin, destination, route, description of shipment, amount charged, and other information needed for the transportation service, and forwarded to the carrier's representative at a transfer point or destination.

way station In a telegraphic network, one of the stations in a multipoint system.

when-issued trades A situation in which securities are traded before they are issued. The trade is not valid if the securities are not issued.

wholesale price index A statistical measure compiled monthly which compares the price changes of a large group of commodities (weighted by their relative importance) to prices in a base year.

wholesaling The activities of a middleman when selling goods or services to those who are buying for resale or business use. *See* distributor.

Wide Area Telephone Service (WATS) A communications link allowing the user to telephone certain bands or zones for a flat monthly service charge.

wire house A member firm of an exchange maintaining a communications network linking either its own branch offices, the offices of correspondent firms, or a combination of such offices. *See* tie line.

withholding Deductions from salaries or wages, usually for income taxes, to be paid by the employer in the employee's name to federal, state, and local tax authorities.

without recourse A specific endorsement on a document stating that the endorser is not liable for events which may occur after the date of the endorsement.

word processing An automated process of storing and manipulating text data in an information system. Data can be edited automatically, added, changed, or deleted and printed on remote terminals in a variety of ways. *See* text editing.

work area A place of storage in a computer calculation, used to retain intermediate results of the analysis.

work cycle A series of sequences needed to perform a task or job, and yielding a unit of production.

working capital Current assets minus current liabilities. Liquid assets available for the normal conduct of business.

working capital ratio Ratio of current assets to current liabilities. It is commonly used to indicate a company's financial position.

work-in-process Partially completed or finished product.

work load The assigned amount of work to be completed in a specific period of time.

work measurement A technique for establishing the relationship of the quantity and quality of work performed and the human or machine resources used.

workmen's compensation insurance An employer's liability contract covering all those liabilities imposed on an employer by the state workmen's compensation act, and applicable to accidents and occupational diseases for which an employer may be held legally responsible but which are not covered by the state workmen's compensation act.

workmen's compensation laws State laws which provide for fixed awards to employees or their dependents in case of industrial or work-related accidents. *See* going and coming rule.

work order An internal document of a firm which authorizes the performance of a specific task or job. Items such as job number, location, and other specifications appear on the document.

work sampling In manufacturing, a technique of work study and measurement, conducted under the direction of industrial engineers, in which a series of measurements of time/

output relationships, or of observations of the work activity, are made at random intervals of time. The technique is used to determine manpower requirements for a particular phase of production or processing.

wraparound A mortgage which permits a lender to advance funds to a borrower in excess of an existing first mortgage without requiring the retirement of the existing mortgage.

W-2 form A document that all employers must give to their employees. The form shows the dollar amounts of wages and other compensation paid to the employee, contributions to Social Security, federal taxes withheld, state taxes withheld, if any, and other pieces of information.

written contract A contract in writing, which usually has a binding effect and is enforceable by law.

Y

yankee bond A foreign bond issued by a company or government in the United States market, payable in dollars and registered with the Securities and Exchange Commission.

yellow-dog contract An employment contract by which an employer requires an employee to sign an instrument promising as a condition for employment that he will not join a union and stating that he will be discharged if he does join. These contracts are illegal.

yield The internal rate of return on a stream of cash flows; cash yield is cash flow divided by book value; the dividends paid, divided by the number of outstanding shares of common stock at the end of the year.

yield curve A graphic description of the interest rates in the financial markets, showing the relationship of various yields to maturities of a variety of securities with different credit ratings.

yield to maturity The rate of return on a debt instrument held to maturity when both interest payments and the investor's capital gain or loss on the security are factored into the calculation.

Z

zero-based budgeting Budgeting in which enterprise programs are divided into defined units comprised of goals, activities, and required resources, and costs are calculated for each unit from the initial steps required to put the program in operation. *See* program budget.

zoning A geographic division of an area, designating sections as residential, commercial, industrial, agricultural, or mixed. Each division carries with it building, design, and subdivision standards and requirements. By creating and enforcing zoning laws, governments develop planning guidelines for the growth of an area.

APPENDIX
Business Slang and Informal Idioms

ad hoc For a special purpose; i.e., a committee set up to study a particular problem.

a mover and shaker A person considered by others to have the ability to serve as a catalyst and get things done.

annual review A regular management and salary review, conducted by a supervisor of the subordinates under his direction. Such reviews could lead to promotion, dismissal, early retirement, and other events.

ASAP As soon as possible; in corporate correspondence almost all letters and memoranda having the slightest urgency carry this designation.

bcc Blank carbon copy; copies of most business letters and other forms of communication are sent by the writer to persons other than the addressee without the letter's recipient knowing about it.

bottom line An objective and a goal of business managers, who are less concerned with the process of production or service delivery than with the revenues and profits expected and actually generated from an activity. *See* process oriented.

break even The minimum level of sales where revenues cover fixed and variable costs of production. The owners of a company cannot continue an operation after a period of time unless revenues are at least at the break-even level. *See* break-even point.

by the book A management or enforcement practice which follows the formal guidelines and regulations laid down by an organization. This rigid concept in certain situations introduces outmoded practices, delays, and disagreements.

cc Carbon copy; a standard administrative practice of sending open carbon copies of a correspondence to persons involved with certain aspects of the communication in question. The greater the number of people receiving copies, the more diluted and time consuming is the decision-making process, and the less likely the decision or event will ever take place.

C.E.O. Chief executive officer, the person who usually holds the power in a corporation.

C.F.O. Chief financial officer of a company.

committee meetings The most common form and arena of decision making within organizations.

corporate climber A person who strives to the highest level in the hierarchy. *See* risk taker.

corporate infighter An ambitious person who will not only work hard but also attempt to improve his or her position by manipulating the internal political structure of an organization.

creative financing A hybrid financing technique combining several areas of finance, such as corporate bonds and mortgage securities, to create the mortgage-backed bonds.

de facto Something which exists with or without prior approval.

de jure Something which exists according to the law.

don't rock the boat An attitude of certain persons in an organization who prefer to stay in their jobs or positions, and are willing to trade off the burden of certain problems of the work environment for job security. *See* team player.

ex post facto Refers to subsequent actions which have no impact on prior events.

fallback option A businessman usually has an alternative course of action in the event his most optimal and highly preferred selection doesn't materialize. *See* tactics.

field rep A salesman with some limited management responsibility.

F.Y.I. For your information; a common abbreviation on memoranda prepared in bureaucratic organizations.

get a leg up on the competition Any action or event which causes a person or firm to take a temporary leadership position over a competitor or a group of competitors within the same market or industry.

grapevine The informal network of communications within a company. *See* rumor mill.

growth area A section of the firm's business which is most likely to experience rapid expansion and provide a strong revenue base and career opportunities for a person. Also, a particular industry which exhibits these characteristics.

head hunter A personnel agent or consultant responsible for recruiting middle- and high-level executives. *See* raiding.

Horatio Alger story Rags to riches; generally a description of a person who has successfully made his way to the top of an organization, profession, or other area of endeavor in spite of a poor background, great handicaps, and/or enormous odds against his success.

in limbo A state of suspension of an activity, such as a decision which may be postponed until further information is obtained on a situation. *See* under review.

input Information or data source used in a decision-making process.

in transit When a person or product is unavailable or temporarily lost, he or it is considered to be in transit.

just-the-facts A phrase used to describe the need to save time and to eliminate paraphrasing, emotional outbursts, or editorializing when describing a set of events or plans.

ladder of success An opportunity or event which allows a person to rise to eminence.

lateral move A change of job or position with no immediate increase in salary or responsibility.

lay it on the line A firm statement of requirements, policies, and actions required in a situation, usually during a negotiation process.

lay our cards on the table A frank and comprehensive discussion conducted by parties involved in negotiations.

leadership potential A performance-oriented person with a high probability of success in a managerial context. The person may or may not also be competent.

managing people The skills required to motivate, supervise, and discipline persons in hierarchical organizations.

marriage of convenience Mostly a temporary arrangement between persons or firms, based on certain perceived needs or expectations.

meeting of the minds An agreement or consensus reached after a period of negotiations; a verbal or written contract.

memorandum A written understanding of, or direction for, a business, political, personal, or other project.

memo to the file A form of record keeping of information pertaining to a set of facts or decisions. The information in the memo may or may not ever be used.

mom-and-pop operation A small company, managed by family members and limited in its ability to expand due to lack of outside capital, management talent, and product diversification.

Murphy's Law The assumption that if it is possible for something to go wrong, it will go wrong.

number cruncher A person who is involved mainly in financial, computer, accounting, and statistically oriented tasks without always knowing the broader issues involved with the numbers. *See* quantitatively oriented.

off budgetary target Not meeting the revenue or cost estimates and objectives set out at the beginning of the budget year.

one-upmanship Interpersonal bickering in which persons try to outperform one another by making relatively trivial and insignificant gains or points.

on target Meeting the goals and objectives set out at the start of the planning period.

options Alternative courses of action that developed through the use of available resources.

out of town The inability to find a businessperson in his office for an extended period of time is usually attributed to his being "out of town."

output Any result which is obtained or available from certain decisions or courses of action.

out to lunch The inability to find a businessperson in his office during the middle of the day is usually attributed to his being "out to lunch."

over budget A financial result when expected costs exceed initial estimates.

Parkinson's Law The law holds that "work expends so as to fill the time available for its completion." It was formulated to apply to government red tape and bureaucratic inefficiency in Britain, but it is seen now to apply to all organizations.

performance gap A deviation of the expected level of performance from the actual results. The term is usually used in business-management and public-administration contexts.

performance oriented The ability to get things done in a given time-and-resource limitation.

perks Perquisites-benefits received by employees above and beyond normal wages, salaries, and standard fringe benefit packages. Perks may include free trips, an apartment, a car, a personal computer, club memberships, among others.

Peter Principle The basic premise of the study of certain hierarchies which states that "in a hierarchy every employee tends to rise to his level of incompetence."

piggybacking Riding to a better position on the coattails or the success of another party without actually deserving the new position. The term is also used in the field of transportation.

potential A hidden or an apparent ability which needs to be developed over time.

process oriented A person whose main interest is to implement the goals and objectives of an organization without necessarily considering the bottom-line implications. *See* bottom line.

quantitatively oriented A person whose skills and interests are in mathematics, statistics, computer sciences, or accounting. *See* number cruncher.

raiding A common practice among companies of hiring away from one company persons with skills, contacts, and experience which are useful for the other organization. *See* head hunter.

real deal A business transaction which has a high degree of probability of leadng to a losing.

realistic approach A relatively low-risk implementation-oriented decision which could be accomplished within the budget and other requirements of the parties involved.

reporting channel A tool of hierarchiology which formalizes the relationship between managers and subordinates.

risk averter A person who looks for relatively safe approaches and assignments, and keeps a low profile in negotiations.

risk taker A highly visible corporate climber, who takes relatively untried paths and directions in business development, negotiations, and interpersonal relationships. If the person is successful in these new areas, higher rewards usually accrue to him. *See* corporate climber.

RSVP Please reply.

rubber stamping An almost automatic approval of a decision or a course of action, presented to a person in a position of formal but not necessarily actual authority.

rumor mill An informal and sometimes inaccurate network and source of information. *See* grapevine.

Silicon Valley The geographic area between San Francisco and San Jose, California. The primary industry of this area is the manufacture of semiconductors and microelectronic chips out of silicon. *See* microelectronic devices.

SOP Standard operating procedure; used to designate prearranged and preagreed courses of action.

status quo A condition in which everything was or is.

status quo ante A condition prior to the present or past.

status symbol A socially or professionally desirable item, position, or association.

team player A person who works closely with others and respects the hierarchy of his organization. *See* don't rock the boat.

trial and error An approach to problem solving, which may result in failures before the optimal or most reasonable solutions are found.

trial balloon A pilot test of a concept or plan, with the understanding that the pilot approach may be withdrawn or modified according to the initial responses received.

under review Since many decisions are not final, they are usually "under review." *See* in limbo.

visibility A characteristic of persons or products receiving wide exposure or publicity, usually through the media.

Washington syndrome A sociological and social psychological description of the perspective prevailing in the nation's capital, which offers at times a limited focus on political, economic, and cultural affairs and events in the nation. The lack of a grass-roots approach to issues is sometimes an attribute of persons and organizations working in Washington, D.C.

wcb Will call back, a common message resulting from the inability of a caller to reach the desired party.

workaholic A person with a compulsive need to do job-related activities. The quality and level of his performance may or may not be superior to the performance of his colleagues.

work horse A person considered by others, mostly his colleagues, to work long hours in the hope that his work performance and productivity will be noticed by the supervisor and lead to a promotion. At times, the person may not receive his justly deserved reward.

working vacation Most executives do not take real vacations, during which they cut themselves off from office problems, phone calls, and mail; hence, they go on "working vacations."

Business Language in America

Business Semantics—a Definition

The language used in communications involving business matters, commercial products, and transactions is defined as business semantics. This language is a conglomeration of many disciplines, ranging from accounting, taxation, and law to statistics, computer sciences, and psychology (see Figure 1). As with all languages, business semantics performs several basic functions: a descriptive function, in which it transmits information through a delineation of facts and events; an expressive function, in which it relates to the listener or reader the feelings of the language's originator; and a directive function, in which it influences the behavior and attitudes of others.

The need for recognizing business semantics as a unique field was expressed by T. R. Malthus in his volume *Definitions in Political Economy* published in 1827. In it he stated that one of the principal causes of the disagreements among political economists may be traced to the different meanings they gave to the same terms. Hence, he advocated the collection of terms and definitions which best describes facts and situations in current usage. He further recognized the changing nature of the language and the need to revise the terms to make them consistent with evolving developments.

Figure 1. Elements of Business Semantics

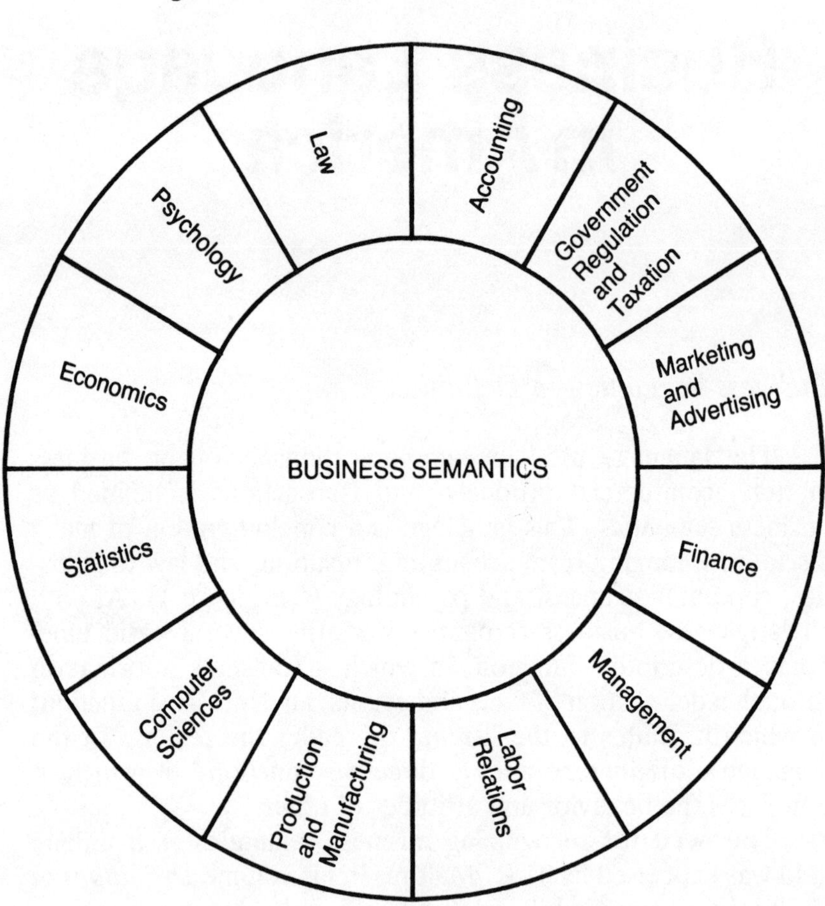

The divergent uses of business language are best demonstrated by the generic word *income.* This word acquires different meanings in the context in which it is used by the accountant, economist, lawyer, or trust executor. *Income* for the economist, *income* under income tax laws, *income* in the determination of national income, *income* to determine the relative rights of remainderman and life tenants held in trust, and *income* to the accountant for a partnership and for a corporation, all vary enormously. Within each field the word takes on added shades of meaning and changes of emphasis. The difference between the use of the concept of *income* by economists and by accountants further illustrates the contrast.

In general, the economist regards *income* as the distributive rent, wages, interest, and profit accruing to each of the four factors of production—land, labor, capital, and the entrepreneur. The accountant, on the other hand, focuses his attention on "profits," as reflected by the entrepreneur in the costs and revenues of a particular business enterprise. Wages, rents, and interests flowing from a business enterprise are *income* to the economist, but the accountant considers them, when they are actually paid, as the costs of production and as expenses. Considering these multiple uses within the language of modern American business, one of the main purposes of this essay is to isolate and document the historical and present-day forces and events that shape the communications tools of our economic and commercial systems.

The Historical Origins of American Business Language

The roots of business interests in North America can be traced back to Colonial times, when a great majority of colonists came from Europe not for the glory of God or the British Empire but to benefit themselves. In many cases, they came bound to indentured labor or contracts drawn up with Colonial promoters; all were expecting material advancement and territorial expansion. The British Crown granted large tracts of land to certain individuals or groups who then hoped to profit from these benefits by selling or exploiting the land.

With the settlement of these areas, the nonagricultural businessman, the merchant, began to play an important role in early American society. His main functions were domestic trading, importing, and exporting. He kept ledgers, took advantage of the transportation, built warehouses, used shipping logs, transacted business in various currencies, and extended credit to his business partners and clients. The tools of communication used by the Colonial merchant were similar to those used in Europe, modified only by the circumstances and business conditions in America.

As Colonial society matured, the need for self-determination became more and more evident. The Declaration of Independence summarized the political and economic concerns of the colonists. The creation of the United States and the adoption of the Constitution established the fundamental political, legal, and economic structure which governed the relationship between the people and the authorities. It formed the basis for orderly trade and commerce in the new country.

In a search for a starting point for economic, business, and commercial dicta, the Constitution of the United States serves as a natural focus. Some scholars believe that the Constitution is essentially an economic document which was written to protect the interest of certain business and economic classes. Charles A. Beard, in his seminal study *An Economic Interpretation of the Constitution of the United States,* argues that the framers of the Constitution helped the interests of four classes of persons: those that owned or had an interest in (1) money, (2) public securities, (3) manufacturing and shipping, and (4) western land held for speculation. These groups, according to Beard, had been hurt by state legislatures and needed the protection and structure of a national government. In contrast, under the new governmental structure, small and medium-sized farmers/debtors were adversely affected, because they couldn't escape from debt obligations, an action which had been possible before through special laws promulgated by state legislatures. While Beard's interpretation of the importance of the economic forces shaping the Constitution has been challenged by such scholars as Forrest McDonald in his *We the People: The Economic Origins of the Constitution,* there is general agreement that the Constitution did establish the legal structure that formed the basis for commerce, trade, contracts, and taxation as the foundations for business relationships and for government regulation of business in the United States.

Among the essential ingredients of business transactions is the ability to enter into valid private contracts. The framers of the Constitution explicitly recognized the importance of this concept through Article 1, Section 10, which contains the basic contracts clause. It reads:

> No state shall . . . pass any . . . law impairing the obligation of contracts . . .

The general function of this Article is to restrain state governments from exerting undue interference with private contracts. The Constitution also contains the Tenth Amendment, which allows the states to exercise policing powers that range from laws regulating economic behavior, business structure, health, and education to other areas requiring the balancing of the protection of private contracts with public welfare.

Another very significant cornerstone of the Constitution is the commerce clause which states:

> Congress shall have the power to regulate commerce with foreign nations, among the several states and with the Indian tribes.

This clause served as the foundation for the establishment of tariffs, customs duties, the Interstate Commerce Commission, and many other institutions that have shaped American business and economic development. These functions and entities created their own jargon, which expanded rapidly as society became more complex during the 200 years since the Constitution was adopted.

From Agriculture to Industrialization

The hundred years following the birth of the United States saw the economic changeover from agricultural dominance to large-scale industrial organizations that employed greater and greater numbers of the American work force. Technological changes, such as the telegraph, tractor, telephone, railroad, and assembly line, established a new language and vocabulary in American business. Scientific management, the grandfather of industrial engineering, placed into common practice the techniques and methods of planning, rebuilding, maintaining, and distributing industrial products. Coupled with the growth of large businesses, labor unions established their position as representatives of the skilled and unskilled workers, and gave birth to a new vocabulary—from *strikes* and *lockouts* to *closed shops* and *arbitration.*

One of the most important industries that encompassed the establishment of the large corporation, the unionized workers, and scientific management was the automobile industry. The main production techniques introduced by the automobile required not only mechanization but a systematic combination of precision, standardization, interchangeability, synchronization, and continuity. Although the continuous-flow operation was first established commercially in 1787 when a grist mill was built near Philadelphia to process grain through a milling process, it was not until the turn of the twentieth century that an actual mechanical production process was established with all the ingredients for a low-cost manufacturing operation.

The automobile dealer franchising and distribution system pioneered the field of consumer-oriented marketing in the United States. As a condition for a franchise, the distributor/dealer agreed to accept the sight draft which came with the bill of lading on each shipment of new cars.

Marketing, Advertising, and Business Usage

The early shaping of the vocabulary of commerce could be attributed in part to the marketing and advertising activities of companies. One of the agents of change in American society was the traveling salesmen who brought information about sophisticated products developed in big cities to remote small towns and agricultural areas. In the early railroad era, these men served as an educational and marketing force, an effort which was paralleled in the 1890s by the direct marketing of consumer goods. The mail-order catalogs of Sears, Roebuck and of Montgomery Ward could deliver goods from their producers to consumers by mail for cash and at a lower price than from other sources. The words and phrases describing the various products and services made their entrances into everyone's daily vocabulary.

As firms grew and became interested in expanding the market share of their products, in introducing new products in the marketplace, or in effecting competition with other companies offering similar products, many companies turned to advertising. The early forms of advertising combined psychology, moral persuasion, creative arts, and basic economics to sell products which, at times, did not meet the expectations of or the promises made to consumers. Nevertheless, advertising and public relations activities have shaped and still are shaping the everyday business jargon used in American society. By 1910, for example, the total advertising expenditures in the country reached 4 percent of the national income, a figure not exceeded to date.

Schooling, Training, and Business Vocabulary

The early forms of education for a trade or commercial position centered around apprenticeships. Although a highly specialized and rather narrow form of education, apprenticeship provided both a forum for learning and usually a guaranteed job after the completion of the understudy period. The trade and vocational schools established around the 1880s attempted to provide useful vocational training in an organized manner. These vocational training schools were opposed by unions for the reason that they believed workers would then be placed in direct competition with recent graduates entering the labor force during high unemployment periods. According to Samuel Gompers, "It is . . . positively wrong for trade schools to continue their turning out botch workmen who are ready and willing at the end of their so-called graduations to take the places of American workmen far below the wages prevailing in the trade."

Prominent educators, led by Charles R. Richards of Teachers College, Columbia University, New York, attempted to convince the unions of the benefits of industrial and technical education. The success of the educators with the unions was slow, and it took from the 1880s to 1910 to develop societal acceptance of the concept of trade, vocational, and technical education. It was in 1910 that the American Federation of Labor joined the National Association of Manufacturers in a joint lobbying program for trade education. At the same time, the Grange and the Association of American Agricultural Colleges and Experiment Stations expanded their lobbying for agricultural studies on all levels. According to a survey of the states conducted in 1910 by the American Association of Labor Legislation, twenty-nine states provided some form of industrial or technical training and education. The skills and vocabulary acquired by the students in these schools were useful in the expanding industrial and commercial sectors of the economy.

Credit Lending Practices, Commercial Transactions, and the Uniform Commercial Codes

Credit facilitates the movement of goods from producers through middlemen such as wholesalers to final consumers. During this process, various legal and business steps are taken to extend credit or to accept credit risk.

In America the extension of credit and the language of credit trace their origins to the settlers of the sixteenth and seventeenth centuries. Bills of exchange were widely used in foreign as well as domestic trade. Merchants in London financed the settlement of Plymouth, Massachusetts, on a seven-year note, which took twenty-five years to repay because of the problems faced by the settlers. The Continental Congress financed part of the American Revolution by borrowing at home and abroad. As an early example of leveraged financing, property confiscated from colonists remaining loyal to England was used as collateral for these loans from other countries.

As the use of credit expanded, the first mercantile credit agency was established by Lewis Tappan in 1841, which was later turned into Dun and Bradstreet, Inc., now known as Moody's

Investor Service, Inc. Terms of trade and discount for near-immediate payments evolved as credit started weighing more heavily on the cash flows of merchants.

The establishment of credit facilities by commercial banks, thrift institutions, insurance companies, finance companies, and other financial intermediaries necessitated the establishment among the states of the Uniform Commercial Code (U.C.C.). The U.C.C. is divided into nine articles and covers the law of sales, negotiable instruments, bank deposits and collections, letters of credit, bulk sales, documents of title, investment securities, and secured transactions. Many of the provisions of the U.C.C. are relevant to credit extension and a wide range of business and commercial transactions. The U.C.C., for example, classifies and categorizes business arrangements and provides the basis for the important elements of the vocabulary of the American business practitioner.

Financial Institutions: Commercial and Investment Banks

As a financial institution, banking has undergone an enormous expansion and growth in the United States. During the period from 1800 to 1920, the number of banks grew from 28 to 30,291. The local, independent bank was at the heart of general commercial finance for nearly two centuries. During the twentieth century, in the money market centers of New York, Chicago, Boston, and San Francisco, the merger of various middle- to large-sized banks created financial giants such as Citibank and Manufacturers Hanover Trust, which started to offer substantial competition to regional and small-town banks. As banks increased in size, the scope of services they provided took on greater complexity.

The main functions of the banking industry are to: (1) participate in the nation's payments mechanism; (2) serve as the key link of transmitting monetary policy from the Federal Reserve System to the national economy; (3) serve as the storage house of riskless financial wealth; and (4) furnish a large proportion of total credit to the economy, affecting the free market credit allocation among sectors. Although involved in nearly every phase of American business activity, commercial banks are not permitted to engage in the distribution of corporate securities and most revenue bonds issued by states and local governments. This latter function is the domain of investment banking firms, also known as broker/dealers.

These banking institutions, in conjunction with the bank regulatory system (such as the Federal Reserve Board, the Federal Deposit Insurance Corporation, the Comptroller of Currency, and the state banking departments), established their own distinct vocabulary, which ranges from federal funds and Regulation Q to average daily balance and stop payment order.

As financial intermediaries between corporations and the public, investment banking firms became important vehicles to secure the capital needs of rapidly growing corporations. With the expansion of financial needs, the investment banking community required greater and greater sources of capital. To meet these requirements and to share and limit the risks of underwriting, investment banking firms formed syndicates that were temporary partnerships or joint ventures established for the purpose of bringing to the market the securities of corporations or state or municipal entities. The language of investment banking kept pace with the growing complexity of financial transactions. From such words and phrases as senior managing underwriter and takedown to penny stocks and the over-the-counter market, this field of finance developed its own idioms and communication forms currently used by the specialists working in these organizations.

Creative Financings

As financial transactions have become more complex and time-sensitive, and as financial managers have moved from maximizing a single objective—i.e., the profit or rate of return—to optimizing multiple objectives, such as tax benefits, credit risks, currency exposure, and reinvestment risks among others, the field of "creative financing" has emerged (see Figure 2). This hybrid field, practiced mostly by sophisticated investment bankers, attempts to structure, implement, and close transactions to

Figure 2. Structural Components of Creative Financings

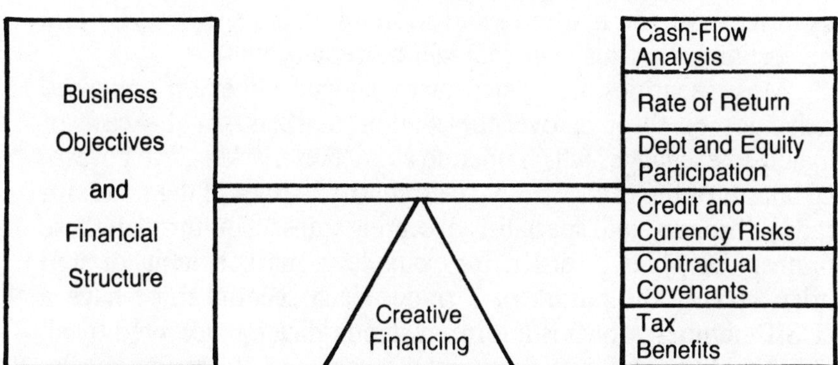

meet multiple business and economic goals and objectives. Also, creative financing is used to merge fields of finance to meet new and nontraditional financing needs. Examples of this are the mortgage-backed bond, the leveraged lease, and the tax benefit sale. All these new financial configurations established a new set of words, phrases, and idioms never before used in this hybrid format. Several financial concepts such as options and futures necessitated the formation of new trading markets, specifically created for the trading of these financial vehicles.

The Language of the Financial Markets

The knowledge of markets requires information on market organizations, pricing trends, supply and demand conditions, the role of middlemen, if any, settlement procedures, and trading practices. This common information classifies almost all markets, including the corporate equity market, the municipal and corporate bond market, the federal funds market, and the commodity markets.

The financial markets are also joined by one main characteristic: they are all involved in the lending of "funds" in one form or another. These funds are lent to the borrower by the lender at a certain price. The price at which a corporate stock sells may imply expectations on current or future dividends and future capital appreciation. The buyer of a mortgage-backed security or corporate debt obligation is most interested in lending his money for the assured yield available from the security and the certainty that his principal will be repaid.

Most securities are traded or exchanged either on organized exchanges or through over-the-counter markets. In the case of organized exchanges which operate as auction markets, the governing boards of the exchanges have established "rules of the road" for traders, brokers, and specialists executing transaction through these forums. The types of order, for example, a market, limit, or stop order, classify the nature of a trade. Each security must have a CUSIP number, which is a form of standardization accepted by all exchanges. On the over-the-counter stock market, similar regulations govern trading practices. These rules and trading procedures are established under federal law by the National Association of Securities Dealers, Inc.

In the international markets, the rules governing trade between nations is in part regulated and maintained by the General Agreement on Tariffs and Trades (G.A.T.T.), headquartered in Geneva, Switzerland. This body monitors the trading, practices, tariffs, and licensing of products flowing through the international markets. Consequently, a uniform language exists in the export-import finance field which permits easy communication between partners operating in these international arenas. A similar universal business terminology binds traders in the international currency markets which allows for the efficient execution of orders among financial institutions or central banks throughout the world.

Government Regulations and Their Impact on Business Semantics

Government has three general functions as it relates to business and industry. All levels of government—federal, state, and local—have a regulatory and policing function that provides for the establishment of laws and regulations for the general benefit of all persons, and attempts to limit the special benefits any particular group may obtain at the expense of others. Government also has a revenue-raising function, which is accomplished through taxation and other forms of revenue generation. Tax policy is also used to provide incentives and indirect subsidies to various groups, industries, and sections of the economy. And finally, government maintains an important position on the expenditure side of the budget for encouraging economic growth, improving the quality of life, and protecting the underprivileged.

Philosophical objectives of governmental public policy shape business actions and the associated business semantics. The implementation of public policy has created its own vocabulary which is the jargon of government contract administrators, environmental analysts, and consumer product safety inspectors. And new government agencies write and design their own unique jargon, forms, and organizational structures.

The formation of the Securities and Exchange Commission (S.E.C.) and the passage of the various securities acts in 1933, 1934, 1935, and 1940 established a new framework of relationships among the corporate sector, the government, and the public. The S.E.C., for example, created standards of full disclosure of information, both financial and nonfinancial, by registrants in connection with new security offerings. It also requires reports from the companies whose securities are traded in the public securities markets. These information requirements, which are captured by Form 10-K and filed by a company with the S.E.C., established the basic information requirements needed by the government.

Several sections of the Securities and Exchange Act contain provisions that specifically prohibit manipulation of securities prices and fraudulent and deceptive practices in the securities market. Language has evolved describing business activities that are fictitious and illegal. Two examples are: (1) "wash sales"—in which one person purchases and sells the same stock at the same time to give the impression of activity in the stock; and (2) "matched orders"—in which transactions between individuals acting in concert to "paint the tape" record a price and give the impression of delivery without a true change of ownership.

The complex regulatory function of local governments is best exemplified through the use of general zoning powers. Zoning means different things to the municipality, the builder, and the homeowner. For the local government, zoning is a tool of both planning and economic development. The builder, however, sees zoning as the means to maximize property values in a manner which will generate the highest and best use of the land. The homeowner, on the other hand, looks to the municipality for protection from unscrupulous land promoters and developers who may destroy the aesthetic and financial values inherent in a property. Here again, the varying shades of meaning for the word *zoning* furthers the notion that language is embedded in the value systems of its users.

The Multinational Corporation, Management, and Homogenized Vocabulary

The twentieth century witnessed the rise of the big corporation, the concentration of power by industrial organizations, and the corresponding increase of the administrative and management personnel required to run and operate these giant enterprises. During the first half of the twentieth century, the ratio of administrative to production workers increased by threefold with the shift to more remote and indirect methods of running production operations. As these hierarchies were established, the need for persons trained in the field of management took on great importance. Simultaneously with the rise of multinational corporations, the techniques and approaches of behavioral sciences, industrial psychology, and organizational development became diagnostic tools used by senior management and outside consultants to solve corporate problems and reformulate management objectives and internal administrative responsibilities.

With the changeover from the family business to the publicly held modern corporation, an overriding requirement for management continuity was established. Modern managers share a common (homogeneous) system of values, training, vocabulary, and other social qualities that are shaped by business schools, corporate management training programs and personnel policies.

Microelectronics, the Information Age, and the Acceleration of History

The last third of the twentieth century is witnessing the rapid infusion of computer- and electronic-based technology. Not only has this established new fields of employment, such as the computer sciences, robotics, bioengineering, and many others, but also it has developed an entirely new vocabulary that has filtered down relatively quickly to daily business usage. Such words as *bionics, minicomputer, Silicon Valley, word processor, WATS line,* and *personal computer* are by-products of the microelectronics/information revolution. These new devices are changing the way people bank, manufacture products, manage offices, and teach in schools. As unnecessary manual and quasi-manual functions are eliminated, the corresponding terminology describing these operations in finance, manufacturing, government, and the service industries has also become obsolete.

Simultaneously with the technological forces shaping society we are also in the front rows of the information age. From all-news radio stations and satellite communications to cable television and financial wire-service information available on home television sets, general awareness of the population for all forms of information—political, cultural, and financial—has noticeably increased. Information, according to one leading scholar, reduces uncertainty. And knowledge allows us to plan and formulate better decisions.

What is the role of business language in this future-oriented society? The medium of communication may change to new technological devices, including electronic mail, video phones, and other systems. Language, with its enormous adaptability, will be reshaped more rapidly than before. New words, phrases, idioms, and related jargon will be formed to meet daily communication needs. Hybrid fields or techniques, such as ergonomics or leveraged leasing, will see the use of words and phrases in new contexts. With the widespread use of minicomputers in office, home, and school, the concepts, tools, language elements, and symbols of mathematics, accounting, statistics, simulation, and modeling will be expanded in everyday interrelationships. Highly technical words used by specialists will become part of the daily business vocabulary. This phenomenon will continue at an accelerated pace.

BIBLIOGRAPHY

Beard, Charles A. *An Economic Interpretation of the Constitution of the United States*. New York: The Free Press, 1941.

Bruchey, Stuart W., ed. *Small Business in American Life*. New York: Columbia University Press, 1980.

Carosso, Vincent P. *Investment Banking in America—A History*. Cambridge, Mass.: Harvard University Press, 1970.

Cherry, Colin. *On Human Communication*. Cambridge, Mass.: The M.I.T. Press, 1957.

Chomsky, Noam. *Language and Responsibility*. New York: Pantheon Books, 1979.

———. *Reflections on Language*. New York: Pantheon Books, 1975.

Cochran, Thomas C. *Business in American Life: A History*. New York: McGraw-Hill, Inc., 1972.

Cremin, Lawrence A. *The Transformation of the School*. New York: Random House, 1961.

Forester, Tom. *The Microelectronics Revolution*. Cambridge, Mass.: The M.I.T. Press, 1981.

Hampton, David R., Charles E. Summer and Ross A. Webber. *Organizational Behavior and the Practice of Management*, revised. Glenview, Ill.: Scott, Foresman and Co., 1973.

Hayakawa, S. I. *Language in Thought and Action,* 4th ed. New York: Harcourt Brace Jovanovich, Inc., 1978.

Leech, Geoffrey. *Semantics.* New York: Penguin Books, 1974.

Lockhart, William B., Yale Kamisar and Jesse H. Choper. *The American Constitution: Cases and Materials.* St. Paul, Minn.: West Publishing Co., 1967.

McDonald, Forrest. *We the People: The Economic Origins of the Constitution.* Chicago: University of Chicago Press, 1958.

Porter, Glenn, and Harold C. Livesay. *Merchants and Manufacturers.* Baltimore: The Johns Hopkins University Press, 1971.

Previts, Gary John, ed. *The Development of SEC Accounting.* Reading, Mass.: Addison-Wesley Publishing Co., Inc., 1981.

Rae, John B. *The American Automobile.* Chicago: University of Chicago Press, 1965.

Robinson, Roland I., and Dwayne Wrightsman. *Financial Markets: The Accumulation and Allocation of Wealth.* New York: McGraw-Hill, Inc., 1974.

Sylla, Richard. *The American Capital Market 1846–1914.* New York: Arno Press, Inc., 1975.